D0044226

Also by Joe Queenan

Imperial Caddy

If You're Talking to Me, Your Career Must Be in Trouble

The Unkindest Cut

Red Lobster, White Trash, and the Blue Lagoon

Confessions of a Cineplex Heckler

My Goodness

Balsamic Dreams

TRUE BELIEVERS

TRUE BELIEVERS

THE TRAGIC INNER LIFE OF SPORTS FANS

JOE QUEENAN

HENRY HOLT AND COMPANY • NEW YORK

Henry Holt and Company, LLC
Publishers since 1866
115 West 18th Street
New York, New York 10011

Henry Holt® is a registered trademark of
Henry Holt and Company, LLC.

Distributed in Canada by H. B. Fenn and Company Ltd.
Portions of chapters 1, 4, and 7 have appeared in different form in *GQ*.

Library of Congress Cataloging-in-Publication Data
Queenan, Joe.
True believers : the tragic inner life of sports fans / Joe Queenan.
p. cm.
ISBN 0-8050-6979-8
1. Sports spectators—United States—Psychology. 2. Sports—United States—Social aspects. 3. Queenan, Joe. I. Title.
GV715.Q54 2003
796—dc21 2002191911

Henry Holt books are available for special promotions and premiums.
For details contact: Director, Special Markets.

First Edition 2003

Designed by Kelly S. Too

Printed in the United States of America

10 9 8 7 6 5 4 3 2 1

To travel hopefully is a better thing than to arrive.

—ROBERT LOUIS STEVENSON

No, it isn't.

—ANY RED SOX FAN

CONTENTS

Prologue	1
1: Fans Who Love Too Much	19
2: Fans Who Know the Score	39
3: Fans Who Run in Front	65
4: Fans Who See Green	89
5: Fans Who Misbehave	113
6: Fans Who Are Short	135
7: Fans Who Get an Earful	155
8: Fans Who Just Enjoy It	175
9: Fans Who Walk Away	195
10: True Believers	213

TRUE BELIEVERS

PROLOGUE

LABÉCÈDE IS AN EXHAUSTINGLY BEAUTIFUL VILLAGE IN the south of France, founded in the early twelth century, roughly 768 years before the Philadelphia Phillies played their first game. The picturesque hamlet of perhaps 375 souls is situated in the rugged Montagnes Noires, the very heart of the Lauragais district where the Albigensian Heresy erupted in the year 1167. Not far away lies the historic city of Béziers, where a French monk, asked by his troops for guidance in distinguishing devout Christians from apostates, blithely remarked, "Kill them all; let God sort them out." Ninety minutes to the south, in the shadow of the Pyrenees, stands Montségur, the last heretic stronghold, where in 1244, 215 holdouts chose to be burned alive rather than abjure their faith. It was an appropriate place for a twenty-five-year-old baseball fan to spend the summer, because supporting the Phillies was exactly like worshiping the Albigensian god: no good would ever come of it, and before the ordeal had run its course, immense pain would be inflicted.

In August 1976, I was in Labécède writing a novel, and things were looking peachy dandy. For me, Jimmy Carter's election notwithstanding, 1976 was an astonishing year replete with hope and promise. I had scraped together the money to move to France. I had started my career as a writer. And the Phillies were making their move. Every day I would rush out to get the *International Herald Tribune* and marvel at their latest exploits. Dismantling every team they faced, they were seemingly in position to win the most games since the 1954 Indians. But the season had another intriguing plot line. First baseman Dick Allen, who had been Rookie of the Year on the 1964 Phils team that blew a six-and-a-half-game lead with just twelve games to go, had left the squad in 1969. By that point, he'd had quite enough of Philadelphia racists, and Philadelphia racists had had quite enough of him. Now, after wandering in the wilderness for several years, Crash Allen was back in the City of Brotherly Love. Here was a chance for the Phillies to reaffirm one of those classic old sports clichés, that baseball is not just a game of inches but a game of redemption. By toting home the pennant they had tossed away a decade earlier, and by healing all those festering racial wounds (starting with the city's abysmal treatment of Jackie Robinson when he first broke into the majors in 1947), the team had an opportunity to banish those old demons forever.

Adding to the abundant mythological flavor of the season was the fact that 1976 was the one hundredth anniversary of the National League, which had played its first game in Philadelphia on April 22, 1876. It was also the centenary of Custer's Last Stand, in which the perennial underdogs, the Sioux and the Cheyenne, had put the kibosh on their hated rivals, the Long Knives, and the one hundredth anniversary of the James Gang's disastrous raid on the Northfield bank, where a hastily convened throng of vastly underrated local farmers had peppered the Long Riders with a whole passel of buckshot. Thus, all the astrological configurations were in place for a radiant Phillies triumph that would reward long-suffering fans for a century of brutal disappointment.

One sweltering morning I received a letter from one of my closest friends announcing that playoff tickets would soon go on sale, and that if I wanted to attend the series against the rampaging Big Red Machine, I should let him know quickly. This put me in a bit of a bind. I had gone to France with the specific intention of writing the Great American Novel and was pretty much determined not to return to the United States until I had. The book I was working on dealt with a young college biology student who, through a series of dangerous skin grafts and appendage transplants involving a frog, succeeded in turning himself into the highest-leaping, greatest basketball player of all time. Needless to say, the novel liberally borrowed from both *The Strange Case of Dr. Jekyll and Mr. Hyde* and *The Fly* and ended with the hero missing a championship-winning dunk because he was diverted by a scrumptious insect that happened to fly past as he was poised to begin a windmill jam. If I was truly serious about remaining in France until the Great American Novel had been written, it was unlikely I would be home in time for the National League playoffs.

Further complicating matters was the fact that I had just begun living with an Englishwoman who would soon become my wife. At the time, we were trying to decide whether to remain in the south of France or set up shop in rural England. As neither of us had much money, finding jobs was a pressing concern. In the middle of one of our conversations comparing and contrasting the splendors of the Dordogne with the delights of the Cotswolds, I happened to recap the entire history of the Philadelphia Phillies, indicating that wherever we decided to settle down, an October detour to the Delaware Valley would be unavoidable.

To this day, I am surprised at how well she took this news. Although she was by no means enthusiastic about this trip to the States, particularly in light of our cash-flow problems, she could understand why I would feel compelled to attend the playoffs because her father and brother had been fervent supporters of the Arsenal football club, the plodding underachievers immortalized by Nick Hornby in *Fever Pitch*. Had my wife not been exposed to delirious fan behavior at an early age, I doubt very much that she would have made the trip. Much less married me.

Unlike Hornby, I was not the kind of fan who needed to take up residence in a house right down the street from my team's stadium, nor was I the kind of fan who would piously abstain from going away for the weekend because it would involve missing a home game. I was a fan, not a fetishist. But I was the kind of fan who knew that when his team had a chance to win their first pennant in his entire life, it was time to go home to cheer them on. Even if home was 3,500 miles away.

The *Rocky* movies are set in South Philadelphia, within walking distance of the sprawling sports complex where the Phillies, Eagles, 76ers, and Flyers all ply their trades. In the original *Rocky,* a plucky but maladroit underdog from the streets of Philadelphia gives the heavyweight champion of the world the fight of his life. In *Rocky II,* he actually takes the title, as he does in *Rocky III* and *Rocky IV* and, for all I know, *Rocky V.* But movies are not like real life, whereas South Philadelphia is. By the time my wife and I surfaced in the City of Brotherly Love, the Phillies had squandered all but one and a half games of their once massive lead over the Pirates and barely won the division. Riven by dissension, torn apart by racial animosity, the fatally wounded team crawled into the playoffs, where they were promptly annihilated by the Redlegs, three games to none. Nineteen sixty-four was not avenged; the echoes of the Whiz Kids were not stirred; Dick Allen did not put the team on his back and carry it to victory; the storybook ending did not materialize. In the game I attended with my wife and friends, the Phillies carried a 2–0 lead into the sixth and were then dispatched 6–2. Dick Allen never played another game for the Phillies.

A COUPLE OF YEARS AGO, I FOUND MYSELF TRAPPED AT the edge of the runway on an airplane at Chicago's horrid Midway Airport, waiting to take off for La Guardia. The delay lasted three hours. Idly, I bantered. The young man sitting next to me said the delay did not bode well for his first trip to New York City. Though I bow to no man in my affection for the Windy City, I assured him that the delay was well worth the wait: New York, New York would be everything he expected it to be—and more.

We spent the next five hours chatting. Born in Chicago, the young man was around twenty-three; he drove a flower truck; he wished to clear up a few points about the state of affairs in Gotham. Specifically, he wanted to know if the respective fans of the New York Yankees and the New York Mets hated each other.

Prefacing my remarks with the caveat that I was not a native New Yorker, I told him that, based on twenty-five years of self-imposed, career-advancing exile in Manhattan and its northern suburbs, I felt it was safe to say that Mets fans hated Yankee fans with a pathological ferocity not unlike what the Palestinians feel for the Israelis, whereas Yankees fans merely viewed Mets fans as a nuisance. I qualified my reply by noting that in using the term *nuisance,* I was not referring to something dangerous, like famished rats or meningitis-bearing raccoons in the attic. In the eyes of Yankees fans, both the Mets and their adherents were more of a pathetic inconvenience, like lint or shih tzu hairs. Since many Yankee fans were occupants of the very lowest rungs of the New York social ladder, this derision was triply infuriating to the Mets faithful.

Inevitably, our conversation segued into a discussion of the curiously asymmetrical relationship between the Chicago White Sox and the Chicago Cubs. Without hesitation, my traveling companion announced that he despised the Cubs and their sanctimonious fans and their overpraised stadium, and had never enjoyed himself more in his entire life than during a recent interleague game at Comiskey Park in which scores of Cubs fans were pummeled into submission. He went on to explain that his antipathy toward the Cubs was typical of the South Chicago milieu in which he traveled. For him, the Sox's taking two games out of three from the haughty, officially beatified Cubs made the rest of the season completely irrelevant.

This was hardly a healthy frame of mind to be in. At the time of our conversation, the Cubs were solidly in first place, a most uncharacteristic position. Meanwhile, the White Sox were mired in yet another of their irrelevant seasons, buried in fourth place, twelve games behind the surprisingly animate Minnesota Twins and the resilient Cleveland Indians. Their best player was out for the season; their best pitcher was on the disabled list; and all this misfortune had come on the heels of a cruel whitewashing by the Seattle Mariners in the first round of the previous season's American League Champion Series. The White Sox, as had so often been their fate, were playing out the string. In July, mind you.

None of this had done anything to dampen the young man's enthusiasm for his team. He loved the Sox. He loved Comiskey. In his unbridled passion for the South Siders, he was aided immeasurably by not actually knowing that much about the franchise. For example, he thought the Black Sox scandal took place in the nineteenth century and involved a franchise called the Black Sox. It did not. He was also under the impression that the Sox had won the pennant at some point in the 1980s. They had not. He was equally sure that the

Sox had captured the flag sometime back in the 1960s. This was also untrue. If you go out and rent the videocassette of the original *Ocean's 11,* you will be treated to an entertaining black-and-white newscast that precedes the film. Featured in the footage are the defending American League champions, clowning around in spring training. *Ocean's 11* was made in 1960, a year after the White Sox won their last pennant. In other words, the White Sox last appeared in the Fall Classic during a period when Americans still voluntarily paid to see Sammy Davis, Jr. movies.

That was a long, long time ago.

As we conversed, I began to reflect upon the similarly dismal legacy of my own beloved ball club. Losing the highest-scoring World Series game in history 15–14. At home. Blowing a 5–2 ninth-inning lead to the Dodgers and losing game 3 of the 1977 National League playoffs because the manager forgot to put a defensive substitute into left field. Losing the 1978 playoffs because Garry Maddox, one of the greatest defensive center fielders of all time, dropped a routine fly ball. Going ninety-seven years without winning a World Series. Going, respectively, thirty-five, thirty-two, and thirty years at a time without even appearing in the World Series. Going one entire century without winning their first pennant in their own stadium in front of their own fans. And, of course, the monumental disgrace of 1964.

Unlike the Cubs and the Red Sox, whose traditions of ineptness had conferred a carefully manicured aura of nobility upon them, the Phillies occupied no similar place of honor in the bosom of the American people. They were the last

National League team to integrate; they had pulled off the biggest tank job in history; they were, statistically speaking, the least successful franchise in the history of the sport. On the other hand, the White Sox weren't much better. They had not won a World Series since Pershing graciously returned Lafayette's favor. They had not appeared in a World Series since the year Batista left Cuba. The most famous player in the entire history of the franchise was an illiterate rustic who helped throw the 1919 World Series. And they played in a crummy stadium in a crummy neighborhood in the same city as Wrigley Field, baseball's official Vatican, Mecca, El Dorado, Avalon, Valhalla.

As I assessed the plight of my traveling companion, I was afflicted by dueling emotions. On the one hand, it was wonderful to see that twenty-three years of disappointment and disgrace had not dimmed the lad's enthusiasm for his underachieving ball club. On the other hand, the young man really didn't know what he was getting into. Take it from an old hand, kiddo, I warned him, rooting for teams like the White Sox and the Phillies was the Vale of Tears, the Stations of the Cross, the Crown of Thorns, the Bataan Death March, and the Babylonian Captivity all rolled into one.

My words fell on deaf ears. He didn't see it that way. Not for a moment had it ever occurred to him that committing himself to a lifetime as a White Sox supporter might be a bad bet. My heart was heavy; I knew that as his life ran its course, and his days dwindled down to a precious few, he was going to find out that seeking happiness as a White Sox fan was like seeking happiness as a blind, tubercular serf.

■ ● ■

IT WOULD SEEM ALMOST IMPOSSIBLE TO DO SOMETHING your entire life without knowing why, yet this is what most sports fans do as a matter of course. It's perfectly clear why people root for the Yankees and the Lakers: the return on investment is relatively high, and the vicarious sense of achievement generated by associating with these teams is priceless and can at least partially compensate for a rotten job, a horrible marriage, a receding hairline, a tiny brain. These fans know exactly what they get out of the arrangement.

But what about the pitiful souls who root passionately for accursed poltroons like the Red Sox, the Cubs, the White Sox, and the Phillies? Why would anyone organize his emotional life around mountebanks like the Cleveland Cavaliers, the San Diego Padres, and the Phoenix Suns, none of whom have won a single championship in their entire history? Is it purely a tribal thing? (Well, the Incas were a tribe and look what happened to them.) An attempt to maintain contact with one's long-vanished childhood? Does it signify a need to believe in fairy tales, in which the tormented, despised underdog, after decades of abject failure, finally enjoys a flickering moment of shining glory? Or is it simply proof that men would rather watch *any* sporting event than interact with their wives and children?

I have often told friends that if my teams were stocks, I would have sold them a long time ago. The Eagles last won a championship in 1960, the Flyers in 1975, the Phillies in 1980, the 76ers in 1983. And while these hiatuses are excruciating, they are hardly of historic magnitude. The Cubs last won in 1908, the Red Sox in 1918, the White Sox one year earlier. The Buffalo Bills, Atlanta Falcons, and Minnesota Vikings have never won a Super Bowl and almost certainly never will. The Chicago/St. Louis/Phoenix Cardinals once went fifty years without winning a playoff game, the New York Rangers fifty-four years without winning a Stanley Cup. Yet their fans adore them.

This book seeks to address several serious issues. One, why do people persist in a massively time-consuming activity that inexorably leads to inordinate misery? Two, how does the experience of the big-city fan differ from that of the fan in Cleveland, Charlotte, Sacramento? Three, given that a huge number of men basically squander their lives watching sports, what is the corresponding activity that women resort to in an effort to squander their lives? (Actually, we'll get that one right out of the way: shopping for footwear.) Finally, is it possible to scale back one's passions and become a casual fan? Is it possible to give up on sports forever? Has anyone ever succeeded in doing this? Is his number listed?

By and large, men do not even think about why they follow their teams. When pressed, they will say it is a way of letting off steam. *Hey, fellas, let's watch the Houston Oilers blow a 35–3 lead in the AFC playoffs to the Bills and let off some steam.* Or they will say it is fun. *Hey, fellas, let's watch the Expos battle the Marlins and have some fun.* Or they will say it's in their blood. *Yes, but so is Lyme disease.* Still others conjure up the brooding specter of testosterone, insisting that sports is a male distraction designed by Mother Nature to give men something they can argue about without resorting to physical violence. But not all males distract themselves this way. And conversing about sports frequently leads to violence. Besides, as a distraction, sex is a much better use of one's time: it is less expensive, you get better seats, you're allowed to smoke if you want, and you can do it indoors in December.

When I speak of sports fans, let me be clear: I am not talking about those preening "super fans" who boast about attending 640 consecutive Notre Dame games—always wearing the same grimy sweatshirt—or who refuse to marry a woman unless she can name the backup quarterback on the 1957 Baltimore Colts team. Fans like this are clowns. Young guns are particularly annoying: they paint their faces; they work on their doo-rag; they vogue the tattoo; they make sure they get the earring just right. Why not dab on some mascara while you're at it, girls?

Cavilers and naysayers may challenge this view: Aren't you the guy who abandoned the fleshpots of Provence to come home to see the Phils lose game 2 of the 1976 National League playoffs? From crummy seats? With your soon-to-be-long-suffering wife in tow?

Yes, I did, but I have a valid explanation. *I had to do it.* Nineteen seventy-six was the first time since October 1950 that the Phillies had appeared in the post-season; that was one month before I was born. There was no question of my staying in Europe. I could never have lived with myself if the Phillies had won the first pennant in my lifetime and I had not been there to see it. (True, I missed Woodstock, but you can lie about that.) Years later, had the Phillies won, my teenage son might have asked me, "Where were you when the Phillies won the pennant in 1976?" What kind of self-respecting man could have borne the humiliation of answering, "France." Bora-Bora, perhaps. Bangkok, maybe. Shanghai in a pinch. But not France. Not la Belle France. Say it ain't so, Joe.

LAST SPRING I WAS STANDING IN A LIGHT BUT STEADY drizzle outside the houses of Parliament in London, hoping to get a glimpse inside those august chambers. The queue was mostly made up of Canadians that day. I had a nice chitchat with two women from Ontario. Right next to them stood two men in Marquette University jackets, who appeared to be father and son. The whole time I was gabbing with the Canadians, they never said a word. This struck me as odd because I was clearly an American; I was even wearing a Cubs cap I'd purchased at Wrigley Field the year before. Eventually, I asked the older man if he had the time. He did. I said I was going to wait fifteen more minutes to get in, and then if the line didn't start moving, I would shove off. They retained their arctic distance. I asked if they were from Milwaukee. The boy said he was a student at Marquette, but they were from Chicago. The father then looked at my cap and said, "You're a Cubs fan?"

I was not a Cubs fan, I assured him. Or let me say that I was only a Cubs fan in the sense that all Americans seem to be Cubs fans, intoxicated by the mythology of Wrigley Field, part of whose charm lies in the fact that the clinically inoffensive Cubs play there. (Who could tolerate the Yankees if they not only got to win all those World Series but also got to play at Wrigley? Yeah, verily, God is great; God is merciful.) I explained that I had been to Wrigley four times in my life, I had seen the Cubs win all four games, and in each of them,

Sammy had hit a home run. Yes, I loved the team's mystique. I loved the majesty of the ivy-colored walls. I loved the long shadows of the late afternoon as they stole across center field. But I was not an actual fan.

If the two men were tight-lipped before, they were even less chatty now. Identifying themselves as South Siders, they made it clear that they hated the Cubs, hated their stadium, hated their mythology, and hated their legions of erstwhile fans. That's why they could stand in a steady drizzle in a city 4,000 miles from home and never utter a word to a compatriot who, if the *chapeau*-istic data was reliable, hailed from the same city as they did. They were imbued by a passion, a resentment, a dread, and a tribal revulsion that was almost beyond human understanding. The father had not seen the Sox win a pennant since 1959, when he was probably about seven, too young to appreciate it; he would have had to have been twice his age to have seen the White Sox the last time they won the World Series. The two men had plighted their troth, such as it was, to a franchise besmirched by the greatest scandal in the history of American sports; they were forced to attend games in a charmless stadium in a dangerous neighborhood; and to make matters worse, the structure was named after the ignoble tightwad who was responsible for inspiring the Black Sox to throw the 1919 World Series in the first place, a man so cheap he used to send the players out in dirty uniforms so he could save money to pay for the sportswriters' buffet. Worst of all, they were condemned to life in a city where millions of lemminglike tourists made self-consciously pious pilgrimages to the arcadian groves inhabited by their despised rivals, a woeful franchise that hadn't captured the

Series since Taft took office. So there they were, standing in the rain: cold, tired, damp, bored, refusing to make small talk with a man in a Cubs cap. It was insane. It was absurd. It was juvenile. It was stupid.

This book is dedicated to those two men.

1

FANS WHO LOVE TOO MUCH

IN A DARK CORNER OF MY KITCHEN, RIGHT NEXT TO THE radio, sits a hideous enamel turtle that has not budged from this position since October 1993. During that memorable year, or so I have come to believe, the turtle's uncanny telekinetic powers contributed in some way to the Philadelphia Phillies winning the National League pennant. Every night that season I would listen to the Phils' barely audible broadcast (I live in suburban New York, 125 miles from Philadelphia, so the signal was rather weak) and adjust the turtle's position according to the game situation. Much as I would like to credit Lenny Dykstra's adroit stick work, Curt Schilling's incendiary fastball, and John Kruk's infectious bonhomie for the team's unexpected success that fall, I am now convinced that without the intercession of the enchanted turtle, the Phils would have gotten creamed by the Atlanta Braves.

Though my reptilian talisman was oddly impotent in the face of Toronto's big bats in the ensuing World Series, and has been completely dormant ever since, I have never ceased to be grateful for the yeoman service it provided during the Phils' march through Georgia in the National League Championship Series that year. Moreover, I am firmly convinced that one day the turtle will reemerge from its paranormal slumber and bring the Philadelphia Eagles that long-awaited Super Bowl victory.

In the meantime, I have begun to see a therapist.

It was a long overdue decision. After years, perhaps decades, of denial, it had finally become obvious to me that an unhealthy obsession with sports was having a devastating effect on my otherwise perfect life. I loved my job, I loved my family, I loved my house, and my friends were no worse than anybody else's. The only thing out of kilter in my sunny existence was my addiction to sports. I watched too many games, listened to too many games, read about too many games, and argued about too many games.

Were it merely a question of following the teams I loved (while secretly believing that ordinary household items possessed supernatural powers that could affect the outcome of games being played 125 miles away), this would not have been a major problem. But I did not limit my passion to the Phillies, Eagles, Flyers, and 76ers. At least half my time was spent watching witching-hour games between teams I had no emotional connection with one way or the other. The Phoenix Coyotes. The Tennessee Titans. And yes, even the Columbus Blue Jackets.

What made things even worse was that I wasn't a gambler. It made sense to stay up till all hours of the night if you had SMU by six over Rice in the office pool. But what person in his right mind would cancel all his appointments just so he could watch Old Dominion plaster the Citadel without having a little something riding on the game?

One day I sat down to calculate how much of my adult life had been wasted on athletic events. Carefully differentiating between time spent watching sports and time spent on ancillary activities such as arguing about sports, I came up with the following jaw-dropping figures.

- Time spent watching teams I love: 7 years
- Time spent watching teams I hate: 4 years
- Time spent watching teams I don't care about: 4 years
- Time spent arguing, often with complete strangers, about who was better, Wilt or Bill Russell, etc.: 3 years
- Time spent sleeping: 9 years
- Time spent on marriage, kids: 6 years
- Time spent on eating, theater, laundry: 1 year
- Time spent on work: 39 weeks

The numbers chilled me to the marrow. Although I was reasonably happy with the way my career had turned out so far, it was clear that the many years I had wasted watching sports was time I could have spent trying to close the yawning talent gap between me and Anna Quindlen. Instead, I had pissed away my life watching the Canucks.

More worrying still was the realization that my compulsion had done serious harm to my family. Because the teams I supported had not won a championship since 1983, I had spent the last eighteen years of my life mired in one continuous foul mood. My daughter, who was born six months after Moses Malone led the 76ers to the NBA title in 1983, says that she can vaguely recall hearing me chuckle during her first birthday party. But my son, born in athletically fallow 1986, claims that he has never seen me smile.

With these troublesome facts in mind, I decided it was time to enlist professional help. Because I am tight with a buck, and because I was not absolutely sure this approach would work, I did not seek out a top-flight analyst. Instead, I found a cut-rate therapist who had taken out a tiny advertisement in the *Village Voice* classifieds. His fee: forty-five dollars for forty-five minutes of "short-term psychotherapy."

Bingo.

Arriving for my first appointment at the therapist's cluttered, tenth-story Upper West Side apartment/office, I diligently explained my problem. I wanted to be cured of my addiction to sports because it was a complete waste of time and invariably put me in a horrible mood and made it unpleasant to be around me. I vowed that I was now ready to confront my athletic demons the same way I would have addressed an eating disorder or a sexual compulsion or a heroin addiction. The toll it was taking on me was too great. I wanted to kick the habit.

The therapist was a diminutive, kindly Italian-American gentleman in his seventies who cheerfully confessed that he knew very little about sports and had no real interest in the subject. Still, he was no stranger to the sort of compulsive behavior I had described, and honestly felt he could help me. But first he would need to know more about my background.

We spent the first few sessions reviewing my generically abysmal childhood. Perhaps, he obliquely suggested, my implacable, lifelong commitment to the hometown teams was a subconscious response to the fact that my father was always changing jobs when I was young. Perhaps my murderous hatred of front-runners derived from early feelings of being betrayed by my uncle Jerry, a surrogate father and role model who stopped talking to me after I suggested to him that his beloved Richard Nixon was a fascist. Perhaps, we now extrapolated, I refused to stop rooting for mutts like the Eagles because I secretly sought stability and continuity in my life, even if this stability unfailingly culminated in defeat and disgrace.

But this made no sense; I loathed defeat and disgrace. I had always sneered at intellectuals who pretended that there was something gallant about the criminally second-rate Red Sox, forever condemned to play Salieri to the Yankees' Mozart. They had taken their cue from books like *The Boys of Summer,* in which Roger Kahn wrote: "You may glory in a team triumphant, but you fall in love with a team in defeat. Losing after great striving is the story of man, who was born to sorrow, whose sweetest songs tell of saddest thought, and who, if he is a hero, does nothing in life as becomingly as leaving it."

Roger, go to your room.

Far from finding nobility in defeat, I found it distinctly disturbing that the outcome of a single game could suddenly, irreversibly wreck an otherwise perfect day. Fall weekends tended to be the worst. I asked my therapist to consider an example. One evening I took my son to see *The Mummy Returns.* It was an amusing, serviceable sequel to a campy original; we both had a great time at the theater and a nice time at the diner; and when we returned to the house I was still in a cheerful mood: upbeat, confident, optimistic. Then I went into the den and fast-forwarded through a tape of the 76ers getting annihilated by the Raptors while I was out at the movies. Whereupon I began shredding magazines, smashing knickknacks, questioning the meaning of life. Yes, another typical Sunday night *chez* Queenan. And it wasn't even a playoff game.

Another time, in Los Angeles, I spent a paradisiacal weekend with my family going all the places you're supposed to go: Santa Monica Pier, Malibu, Venice Beach, Hollywood, the tar pits, Mulholland Drive, Universal Studios, the Cheesecake Factory, and, most important of all, the rooftop pool. As Sunday evening approached, I could not possibly have been more loose of foot or free of fancy. Then the feckless ne'er-do-well Bobby Hoying fumbled away a sure touchdown on the goal line against the Cardinals, and the Eagles lost another game they should have won. At this point I became so apoplectic, so convinced that life was one vast, terrestrial, personally targeted conspiracy, that my children asked me to leave the hotel room. Forever, preferably. Which I was more than happy to do, given their namby-pamby attitude toward my team.

As I recounted these unnerving anecdotes, the therapist merely listened, nodded, wrote down notes. He was clearly a seasoned professional, a sage and wizened veteran used to dealing with train wrecks like me.

"Maybe you have trouble dealing with euphoria," he calmly

suggested after I told him about the night in college when I got so upset at a St. Joe's Hawks upset defeat by Villanova that I tore a washbasin out of the wall and smashed a mirror into a thousand pieces. "Maybe, watching your team lose is a way of bringing you back down from that state of euphoria."

Gosh, I'd never thought of *that*. Now that I set my mind to it, I realized that ever since I was a little kid my teams had been helping me deal with euphoria by getting massacred in Super Bowls they were favored to win, and blowing insurmountable leads to teams they clearly outranked. Maybe people like me could only thrive in a euphoria-deficient atmosphere, the same way people who were euphoria-tolerant seemed perfectly happy rooting for the Yankees, even though they had to spend their entire lives experiencing the same emotion over and over and over again. Except for that one time when Little Donny Baseball didn't get his ring.

In the weeks that followed, my therapist worked hard to peel away the various layers of neuroses that masterfully concealed what we both hoped was a fully developed personality. We talked about congenital alcoholism, family bankruptcy, and the role the Great Depression had played in shaping my parents' worldview. Much like fourteenth-century peasants who incessantly bellyached about the Black Death, my parents blamed the Great Depression for everything: badly cooked meals, crummy Japanese sneakers whose soles peeled off the second time you wore them, chronic alcoholism. But our conversations always came back to sports.

Looking back through the mists of time, I realized that my heart had first been broken the summer after JFK's death, when the Phils blew a six-and-a-half-game lead by losing ten straight games at the end of the season. In my mind, the 1964 Phils, America's first Irish-Catholic president, and Lee Harvey Oswald were all eternally linked in a Bermuda Triangle of neurasthenic, quasi-aphasic post-traumatic stress. But this still did not explain why I stayed up late at night watching Old Dominion whip on the Citadel.

The direction our conversations took provided me with much food for thought. Inevitably, we returned to 1964, the *annus horribilis.* In every other city in the United States, young people first experienced the devastating trauma of JFK's death on November 22, 1963, but then, just when they thought they would never get over it, the Beatles came out of nowhere and literally saved the world. But for Philadelphia fans, the brief emotional uplift provided by the Fab Four quickly gave way to the catastrophe of late September.

At the time of the collapse, I was attending the Maryknoll Junior Seminary in Clarks Summit, Pennsylvania, a nondescript hamlet roughly ten miles outside Scranton, a dying coal town. I was thirteen years old, I had been in the seminary roughly three weeks, and I already knew that I did not want to be a priest. And I certainly didn't want to be a missionary. The first night, after our parents had abandoned us to the clerics' tender mercies, one of the priests showed some of us a wound he had suffered in a Japanese prisoner-of-war camp during World War II. A second discoursed in grisly detail about the sort of treatment we could expect should we fall into the hands of the dreaded Mau Maus, the merciless Red Chinese, the fiendish Soviets. I was thirteen; I had only entered the seminary because of pressure from my father and even greater pressure from Maryknoll recruiters who'd started "scouting" me at age eight after I foolishly set up a mock "altar" in my bedroom; and I had already decided that I did not want to have my fingertails torn out, my ears cut off, or my sauteed liver fed to passing curs just to impress some omnipotent deity whose existence I now questioned. Viewed with the benefit of hindsight, the Maryknolls were a poor choice on my part; I should have sent my application to the Little Sisters of the Poor.

Meanwhile, the Phillies were blowing the pennant.

I do not know if defeat strengthens your character, but I know that it sharpens your memory. Yankee and Laker fans regularly misremember dates, eras, championships, putting DiMaggio on teams with Maris, putting Bob McAdoo on the 1986 championship team, but not the 1984 one. Less fortunate fans, those in Buffalo, Cleveland, Baltimore, Philadelphia, never forget anything. To this day, I can recall how the Phillies headed down the highway to hell during those last two weeks of September, the whole nightmare starting with a 1–0 loss in a game decided by a Chico Ruiz steal of home, with Hall of Famer Frank Robinson at bat. Yes, *that* Chico Ruiz.

Retroactive memory aids were provided by my mother, who would dutifully cut out *Philadelphia Inquirer* accounts of each game and send them off to me, much the way Spaniards living in 1589 Great Tunbridge Wells used to send their relatives in Madrid six-month-old newspaper accounts of the Armada's latest misfortunes. *Thanks, Esteban; we heard.* The neatly clipped articles would arrive two to three days later, by which point the Cardinals would have excised another two games from the Phillies' lead. Of course, I already knew the outcome of the games; I was the only seminarian from Philadelphia, and many of the other ninety-two students enjoyed waking me in the morning with detailed accounts of the Phils' latest tank job. The last clip Mom sent contained a heartrending quote from backup catcher Gus Triandos, a scrub who had toiled in the wilderness for eleven years since being shipped out of town by the Yankees in the biggest trade in baseball history (seventeen players changed teams). "Some guys want to guzzle the champagne," he told the reporter. "I just wanted a sip."

Me too. What I remember most clearly about that watershed month is that it was my first exposure to the concept of *schadenfreude.* None of the other ninety-two seminarians had any direct stake in the pennant race; none of them were from St. Louis, which eventually won the World Series, or from Cincinnati, which would have taken the flag had the Phils not beaten them the last two games of the season. Most of the students were from obscure burgs with names like Osprey's Redoubt, Wisconsin, or Gideon's Agot, West Virginia, and thus had no stake in the outcome of the pennant race. But they enjoyed taunting me anyway. Those few weeks in the seminary opened a rift between God and me that has never closed; while I am grateful to God for giving me my children, my career, and the ability to dance as if no one was watching, sing as if no one was listening, and eat as if no one was paying, I decided at the time that any deity that would let the Phils lose ten games in a row and then hire ninety-two mean-spirited cocksuckers to help spread His word was going to have to manage without me. I shuttered my religious career right then and there.

My therapist patiently listened to all this rambling, taking voluminous notes. As the sessions continued, I made immense progress toward understanding the nebulous substratum of my meta-etiolated psyche. Unfortunately, this did not help with my addiction. Every week I would arrive at his apartment, revved up because the Phillies had just rattled off a string of wins, and my therapist would ask ridiculous questions about my mother. Or I'd try to explain my empathy for eighty-year-old Beantowners who had wasted their entire lives waiting to see the Red Sox win the World Series (even though I secretly hoped they would never win because jinxes are great for baseball, and the Celtics had already won sixteen championships), and he would counter with questions about my childhood dreams of becoming a priest. Or I would attempt to decode a recurrent dream in which the Devils' resident villain Scott Stevens gets decapitated by a fatal but otherwise clean check by Eric Lindros, and he would thoughtfully inquire about my father's drinking.

Of course, I understood perfectly what was going on. The therapist was trying to get me to talk about my formative childhood experiences and come to terms with a handful of "screen memories" that encapsulated a whole series of events rolled into a single image, thus becoming mental constructs so powerful they blocked out everything else. He was trying to get me to see not only who I was but how I'd gotten that way.

But I already knew who I was. I was the guy who believed that by positioning a small enamel turtle right next to a radio, I could materially affect the outcomes of baseball games being played three states away. I already knew that I was mentally ill. I didn't need a therapist to tell me.

Eventually, it became clear that my therapist viewed my addiction as a symptom of a deeper personality disorder, not as a disorder in and of itself. I, on the other hand, knew that I was crackers. While he wanted me to come to terms with the causes of my dementia, then perhaps deal with the sports issue later, I was more like the guy who shows up at the doctor's office with a detached penis in his hand. *It doesn't really matter how it got this way, Doc. Just fix it.*

One day we had a falling out. The Sixers had blown an eighteen-point lead and lost game 1 of the first round of the playoffs to the decrepit, inferior Indiana Pacers, and the Flyers had been demolished 8–0 by the Buffalo Sabres and knocked out of the Stanley Cup playoffs. I arrived for our session in a black mood.

"How was your weekend?" he asked me.

"Putrid," I told him, citing chapter and verse. "Disgusting. Horrible. The worst weekend ever."

"I find it a little bit hard to believe that you can get that worked up about a baseball game," he told me.

"Basketball," I corrected him. "Basketball and hockey. The 76ers play professional basketball, and the Flyers play professional ice hockey."

"Well, I wouldn't give a rat's ass about a team losing a game like that. That's not the sort of thing that would ruin my weekend."

"What sort of thing would ruin your weekend?" I inquired. "What sort of thing do *you* care about?"

He had his answer all ready.

"Well, the destruction of the rain forest, or global warming, or something like that. Not a basketball game."

It was clear that our therapeutic liaison had reached a serious impasse. Stiffening, I stared at him with an expression of infinite contempt.

"How could you possibly compare the fate of the rain forest to the fate of the Philadelphia 76ers?" I said. "You need to get your priorities straight."

YET IN THE END I FOUND MYSELF POWERLESS TO CALL OFF our increasingly fruitless Wednesday afternoon sessions. Week after week, I faithfully turned up at his office/apartment. Why? Did I honestly believe that if we stripped away enough layers of self-delusion I would eventually isolate the roots of my neuroses? No. Did I seriously believe he could help me devise clever intellectual constructs enabling me to see sports for what it was: a pastime, a diversion, a leisurely distraction of no great consequence? No. Did I really and truly believe he would ever help me get this monkey off my back? No.

Why, then, did I continue going to see him? Simple. From the time I started seeing my therapist, my teams came on like gangbusters. The Phils got off to a great start and by June had an eight-game lead over the Braves. As our sessions rolled along, and the bills piled up, the 76ers continued their magical spring; first, the Pacers fell in four, then the Raptors went out in seven, and then the 76ers outlasted the Bucks. Why, I asked myself, after seventeen years of abject failure had the 76ers suddenly become world beaters?

The answer was obvious: It was because of my visits to the therapist. For whatever the reason, as long as I kept going to see him, the 76ers kept winning. Not to put too fine a point on it, the therapist had replaced my enamel turtle as the unexpendable amulet and all-purpose good luck charm that would fling open the gates to the Promised Land.

Such psychologically questionable behavior is by no means rare. In the otherwise unwatchable film *Celtic Pride,* there is a scene where the veteran hams Dan Aykroyd and Daniel Stern, playing die-hard Celtics fans, force everyone in their section to switch places because they believe it will increase the home team's chance of winning. Shortly thereafter, they ask a man to leave the stadium because he was in Boston in 1986, the year the Red Sox choked away the World Series to the Mets. Stern also expresses relief when his wife asks for a divorce because the last time she packed her bags the Celtics won the NBA championship. In these inspired sequences in a film that is in every other way ghastly, the director hit the nail right on the head. In their more lucid moments, sports fans know perfectly well that they cannot affect the outcome of games by wearing stupid hats, closing their eyes, turning down the sound, smearing the quarterback's face with their thumbs, or asking someone to leave the room. Yet they do it anyway.

Over the course of the years, I have indulged in many overtly superstitious activities. A firm believer in chaos theory—if a butterfly flaps its wings in Beijing, the refs will rule that the Flyers were offside—I act out innumerable game-day rituals. Not drinking the last dregs out of a coffee cup because as long as the beverage stayed in the cup, my team maintained their lead. Only entering the house through the side door, walking backward. Refusing to throw out a lucky Christmas tree until the playoffs were over. Sitting in a particular chair. Taking three trains, two subways, and a bus from suburban New York to Philadelphia on three consecutive Sundays to watch pivotal Eagles games on a "lucky" television set. (The appliance's luck ran out when the Eagles played Dallas.) Telling my son to sit in a particular chair and then refusing to let him move. Sadly, in sixteen years of using my son as an intermittent good luck charm, all I have to show for it is that lone Notre Dame national championship in 1988. Yet I am convinced to this day that had I not spent that entire season squishing my son's pudgy forefinger against quarterback Tony Rice's helmet every time he appeared on the screen, the Irish would have finished out of the money. In this context, it is worth recalling that Shoeless Joe Jackson, whose glove was known as "the place where triples go to die," never took the field without sticking a bunch of lucky hairpins in his back pocket. Look where it got him.

FANS USUALLY HAVE AN AMBIVALENT, BUT BASICALLY unwholesome, relationship with God, their Higher Power, Allah, the Great White Father, what have you. In God's defense, He knows that even if He lets the Cubs win the World Series, it's only going to create a million new atheists in Boston or the South Side of Chicago; He also knows that all those Cubs fans' bottom-of-the-ninth promises to stop drinking or to be eternally faithful to their wives are not going to be honored no matter what measures He takes. God may be cruel, but He is not stupid.

As noted, my own relationship with God started to sour in 1964 and has never seriously improved. Whether complicit or neutral in the nightmarish Phillies meltdown, God has regularly impacted negatively on the fortunes of my teams, taking particular delight in hamstringing the Philadelphia Eagles, often because of needless intrusions into contract negotiations. For example, after ex-Eagles defensive end Reggie White revealed that God had personally told him to sign with the Green Bay Packers in 1993, word leaked out that God had apparently made a similar suggestion to ex-Eagles quarterback Randall Cunningham when he was being wooed by the Minnesota Vikings. It was both baffling and infuriating to me that God should only intercede in difficult contractual discussions *after* players had left my teams. Director Spike Lee hits the nail on the head in his film *He Got Game,* where high school superstar Ray Allen tells Denzel Washington, his jailbird dad who has suddenly got religion, "How come you never hear Jesus being praised in the losers' locker room, then? Huh? They're probably cursing that motherfucker out."

Because the psychoanalytic universe is so vehemently nonsectarian, my therapist and I never got around to discussing religion per se. It wouldn't have made any difference, because as April turned into May and May into June, it became evident that my experiment with psychotherapy was not going to bear fruit. Despite our mutual efforts, I did not cure myself of my addiction to sports, and my therapist's status as a good luck charm did not result in any championships. Still, he was not entirely to blame. When the 76ers were playing the Lakers in the 2001 NBA finals, I was out of town and unable to attend our weekly sessions. Stripped of my human rabbit's foot, I resorted to other measures. The night the Sixers hosted the Lakers in game 3, the pivotal contest they absolutely had to win but did not, I visited Christ's Church at Second and Market in the old historical district of Philadelphia and prayed that

Allen Iverson would score fifty. Christ's Church is a luminous, sun-drenched house of worship built in the early 1700s; it was the church where Ben Franklin, George Washington, and Betsy Ross used to attend Sunday services. It is not an accident that I prayed for Iverson while kneeling in Betsy Ross's pew; deep inside I did not really expect the Sixers to beat the bigger, stronger, better Lakers and did not want to squander the precious occult powers putatively emanating from George Washington's and Ben Franklin's pews this early in my life. I was saving them for a time when I thought the home team really had a chance.

The time may be coming soon. Donovan McNabb and the Eagles were picked by many experts to make it to the Super Bowl in January 2003. If they do, I plan to pray for them in Ben Franklin's pew in the first half, and George Washington's pew in the second. And before I head down to Philadelphia for the game, I intend to put in a visit to my psychotherapist with that hideous green enamel turtle in my pocket. I've already invested about $700 in psychotherapy; this time I'm pulling out all the stops.

2

FANS WHO KNOW THE SCORE

ALBEIT AN ACQUIRED TASTE, AND DESPITE THE FACT THAT Christina Ricci is in it, Vincent Gallo's weird, grainy, low-budget *Buffalo '66* is one of my favorite sports films. A testament to the intransigence of the male primate and the infinite complexity of the human condition, particularly in the Snow Belt, the movie relates the heartrending saga of a dysfunctional Buffalo Bills fan whose mother has never forgiven him for being born during the only AFL championship game the Bills ever won (1966).

Hoping to win back Mom's affection, Junior puts $10,000 on the Bills to win the 1991 Super Bowl and gets hosed. Needless to say, he does not actually have the $10,000. After agreeing to an ultimatum from Mickey Rourke, here playing the *capo di tutti bookies,* that he confess to a crime he did not commit and serve the commensurate jail term—or else "very bad, very evil" things will happen to his family—the surrogate schlemiel gets sprung from the slammer and decides to track down and kill the kicker who missed the field goal that would have beaten the Giants.

Rourke's soliloquy is worth repeating here. As Gallo sits motionless, wordless, pointless on a couch, the fabulously slimy Rourke spells out the predicament the welsher finds himself in.

"Okay, so the story goes like this," he explains in his precise, trenchant, antiseptic style. "One day, this big asshole comes in, he calls up a bet, a $10,000 bet on Buffalo to win the Super Bowl. That's to win, okay? Now, I know what you think, the story's hard to believe, all right. I mean: what kind of an idiot would bet on Buffalo to win a big game like that?"

What kind of an idiot, indeed?

Admittedly, this is a disturbing premise for a movie. Yet the film is imbued with a subtle, delicate, and perhaps even poignant metaphorical truth that can be found in no other sports movie I have seen. Gallo has captured exactly the way most fans feel about athletes who screw up. They want to go gunning for them. Or at least go over to their house and break their windows, the way some vindictive South Jersey fans did the night Mitch "Wild Thing" Williams room-serviced a Series-winning, bottom-of-the-ninth home run to Joe Carter in 1993. This is bad behavior, criminally bad behavior. I do not approve of it. I do not condone it. But I can definitely understand it. Frankly, I believe that only a poor marketing campaign and the presence of Christina Ricci prevented this movie from being bigger than *Gone With the Wind.* Boy, does it ever hit a nerve. In fact, I'm surprised that Vincent Gallo hasn't made a sequel entitled *Twin Cities '98,* in which a crazed fan tracks down the kicker who missed the chip-shot field goal that would have put the Vikings in their fifth Super Bowl a few seasons ago. Ironically, Gary Anderson, who had not missed a single field goal that entire season, was rehired by the Vikings in 2002 because the guy who replaced him was a bum.

I am not arguing that Gallo's character is a positive role model. Fan violence of this nature is to be deplored. But to deny that one has ever seriously contemplated killing the place kicker is to deny one's own humanity. A fan who hasn't at least thought about killing the place kicker is really no fan at all. Or if not the place kicker, at least the holder.

Being a sports fan is first and foremost a question of unbridled passion. Well, passion and rage. Well, passion, rage, and disbelief. In his valentine to his beloved Arsenal football club, the previously mentioned *Fever Pitch,* Nick Hornby discusses the immense vulnerability involved in rooting for a team that does not usually win. Since this is the only situation in which men volunteer to be completely supine and defenseless—okay, almost the only situation—it is my honest belief that without sports, the average man would have no emotional life whatsoever. Marriage is nice, but it's just a phase. Kids can be fun, but they grow up and leave, and a lot of them end up in prison. Money and a career are great, but it's hard to relate to them viscerally. No matter how hard you try, you're never going to find 65,000 complete strangers willing to stand in subzero temperatures cheering for your bank statement.

Though it may come as a surprise to the hoi polloi, there

exists a voluminous body of scientific research seeking to quantify the complex emotional liaisons fans have with their respective teams. These include publications as varied as "On Being a Sore Loser: How Fans React to Their Teams' Failure" (L. Mann, 1974, *Australian Journal of Psychology*), "Emotional Responses to the Sports Page" (D. L. Wann and N. R. Branscombe, 1992, *Journal of Sports and Social Issues*), and "Costs and Benefits of Allegiances: Changes in Fans' Self-Described Competencies After Team Victory Versus Defeat" (E. R. Hirt, D. Zillmann, G. A. Erickson, and C. Kennedy, 1992, *Journal of Personality and Social Psychology*). In these exemplary documents, researchers from divergent cultures and diverse academic disciplines have unearthed seemingly incontrovertible evidence that sports fans hate losing, feel just terrible after a team loses, and can be pretty nasty to other people in the wake of defeat.

These findings mesh seamlessly with the conclusions reached by Debra A. Laverie and Dennis B. Arnett, in their immensely influential study "Factors Affecting Fan Attendance: The Influence of Identity Salience and Satisfaction," which originally appeared in the *Journal of Leisure Research* in 2000. Here the researchers, whose recognition by the Nobel Committee cannot be far off, report that fans are more likely to identify with their teams during the season than during the off-season. I too, in my own experience, have found this to be true. Nevertheless, as a firm believer in the journalistic tenet that even if your mother tells you something is true, you should still confirm its accuracy, I did some of my own footwork here. Conferring with a Green Bay Packers fan who had twice become so ill after a defeat that he could not drive his car home, I asked if he ever had a similar reaction thinking back on those defeats during the spring and summer months. The answer was no. Laverie and Arnett are clearly on to something.

Perhaps the most important work in this area has been conducted by Robert M. Fernquist, of the Department of Sociology and Social Work at Central Missouri State University. In a paper published in the *Journal of the Sociology of Sport Online* in 2001, Fernquist argues that when professional teams relocate (the 1957 Dodgers and Giants, the 1995 Cleveland Browns, the 1997 Houston Oilers), "results indicate that, while homicide rates seem to be unaffected by these moves, suicide rates appear to increase." This is not a disclosure to be taken lightly. That Dodgers and Giants fans would take their own lives should come as no surprise—they got the Mets as a cruel consolation prize—and the self-immolation of devout Browns fans is equally understandable. But a significant upward spike in metropolitan suicides triggered by the demise of the Houston Oilers is a very troubling development indeed.

Speaking as an untrained layman, I must confess to amazement at the nuance and wealth of insight contained in these studies. Although tribalism and the desire to please one's parents, no matter how distant, no matter how dysfunctional, are key components of the fan's psychological disposition, there can be no denying that the desire to win is the single most important component of the spectatorial experience. Even though the Oilers rarely won while they were based in Texas, it was physically impossible for them to win once they had left. And given that there isn't much to do in Houston during the winter, it is surprising that more suicides have not occurred. Philip Roth got it right in *The Great American Novel,* his underappreciated paean to the national pastime, when he wrote, "The sooner we get rid of losing, the happier everyone will be."

SETTING ASIDE THE ISSUES OF HOMICIDE AND SUICIDE FOR the time being, let us examine what it means to be a true fan. My harried therapist once asked if I could delineate my sports philosophy in a concise and economical fashion, if only for the edification of the vulgar. Hey, no problem, Doc. I just happened to have a tattered old slip of paper setting forth the fan canon in my wallet; it had been given to me as a boy by a rakish carny who claimed to have once been Dizzy Dean's grocery boy. It consisted of the following items:

- Never switch allegiances.
- Show some respect.
- Visit the shrines.
- Never give up.
- Never give in.
- Never leave early.
- Neither a front-runner nor a Johnny-come-lately be.
- Accept no substitutes.
- Wait until next year.
- Never turn down tickets to see Jordan.

This is a perfectly adequate set of fan guidelines. It is the sort of sensible, well-thought-out list one might pass on to a precocious tot, an inquisitive debutante, or a snoopy foreigner to provide him with a general idea of what it means to be a fan.

But in the end, these axioms and exhortations do not adequately address the deeper, more intimate, and in some cases less socially acceptable passions of the die-hard sports fan. Here, then, is a supplementary collection of suggestions, mantras, and axioms that cuts through to the very heart of the spectatorial matter.

- *Wear the hat right, doofus.*
- *Never act like you're having a good time at preseason games.* It will only encourage the owners to raise ticket prices.
- *Do not root for people like Anna Kournikova.* She is a charlatan, a fraud, the second coming of the Boz. I don't care how much flesh she shows; stick with the Williams sisters. Serena shows a lot of flesh, too.
- *Be grateful for what you've got, even if you have nothing.* No matter how crummy your team is, pretend to enjoy their foibles. Otherwise, the owners will move the franchise to Columbus, Ohio.
- *Don't pout.* Just because the Yankees aren't involved is no excuse to boycott the World Series. You've already got twenty-six rings; let somebody else drive the car. Besides, those Angels are fun.
- *Be selective about your hero worship.* When Jim Bouton's *Ball Four* was published in 1970, I found it a revelation. Here was a brash, sassy, cocky ex-jock who was willing to demystify the whole athletic experience by treating sports legends without a scintilla of reverence. Now, after a quarter century of listening to athletes who think sports is a joke, I think it is the most dangerous, solipsistic book since *Mein Kampf.* Regardless of all the sleazy revelations about Mickey

Mantle, Mantle is still a god, and Bouton is still a scrub. In one of the book's countless introductions, prologues, updates, Bouton sneers that he would not pay to see a baseball game. A man who would not pay to see a baseball game is not a man I would invite into my house, much less my society.

- *Have the wisdom to accept the things you cannot change.* For example, the outcome of the fifth race at Aqueduct.
- *Attention, lunkheads: gambling is a disease.* Some fans will bet against their own teams, figuring that it is worth losing a bit of cash to see their teams win. More often that not, their teams lose but fail to cover the point spread, so the fans get hit with a double whammy. I would never bet either for or against my teams, as it would make an unbearable situation even worse. It would force me to spend all my time worrying about point spreads and the outcomes of games in other leagues and conferences. I don't care about teams from other leagues and conferences. I have never reconciled myself to the National League's 1969 expansion. I have never seen the Chargers, the Grizzlies, the Marlins, the Rockies, or the Coyotes in person. And I aim to keep it that way.
- *Don't blink or you may miss something historic.* Like Dusty Baker foolishly taunting the Furies by handing Russ Ortiz the ball as a souvenir of what seemed like a Series-winning performance. Like Mookie Wilson's grounder. Like Babe Ruth calling his shot.
- *Don't be a schmuck.* If you are a lifelong Yankees fan but never went to Ebbets Field, have the good sense to keep it under your hat. This is like being a lifelong resident of Rome

and never visiting the Vatican. Even if you are a Lutheran, a Muslim, or a practicing atheist, it looks bad on your record.

- *Burn those stats.* Just tell me if you won. *Also sprach Auerbach.*
- *Admit that Rotisserie League baseball is for twerps.*
- *Don't expect the players to be any better than they are.* Be happy that they aren't worse.
- *No doo-rags.* You're not Captain Kidd.
- *Stop bitching about the Yankees.* When push comes to shove, moaning and groaning about the Yankees hegemony is like complaining about August humidity or the *New York Times*'s liberal bias. They are forces of nature; stop banging your head against the wall.

Obviously, those of us who do not support storied, absurdly successful franchises desperately wish that our teams could be cornerstones of our national sports mythology. Sorry, HBO is not interested. The network is busy working on *61, Part II,* the sequel to the Billy Crystal film that chronicles the epic duel between Roger Maris and Mickey Mantle for home run supremacy. Crystal is one of those infuriating New Yorkers who acts as if his passion for the Yankees involves some sort of risk, when in fact saying you support the Yankees is like saying you support the air. Crystal also acts as if the Maris-Mantle story were late-breaking news. I don't know how everybody else feels about this, but I would be more than willing to take a fifty-year sabbatical on the "Today I am the luckiest man in the world" speech and the rest of the Yanks' overdone mythology.

But there's no use losing sleep over it, because it's not going to happen. You only have to be a fan for about four months before you realize that even when something great happens to your team, it is probably not going to be remembered because it didn't happen in New York. The 1966 Orioles shocked the world by sweeping the Dodgers. You never hear about them. The 1929–31 A's were better than the 1927 Yankees. You never hear about them. The 1974–75 Warriors with their bizarre twelve-man squad are one of the most compelling stories in the history of the NBA. You never hear about them. If you want to hear about the 1976–77 Trail Blazers, you're going to have to go to Portland and visit the Oregon Sports Hall of Fame. (It was closed for a private function the day I turned up.) All the folklore of sports is packaged by a Central Planning Commission, whose job it is to persuade the public that spare parts like Bill Bradley were stars and that the competent but unspectacular Knicks teams of the early 1970s are somehow in a class with the Celtics, Lakers, and 76ers. The thing I remember most about those Knicks teams was that Red Holzman took Earl Monroe—the most exciting player on the planet—and neutered him. In a better world *The Boys of Summer* would be about the Mariners or the Indians, and children would grow up watching films like *Damn Padres!* This is not a better world. Ask the folks in San Diego.

But while supporters of the Yankees get most of the good things in life, they do not get everything. One of the most inspiring events in the history of mankind is the Battle of Bannockburn, where the hopelessly outnumbered Scots avenged William Wallace's brutal murder and threw the English out of Scotland for the next 400 years. Yankees fans can never know the elation of such triumphs. As long as they live, they remain the Romans, the Hittites, the Raj. When they use the term *die-hard fan* to describe themselves, they know they are being ridiculous. The longest drought between Yankee World Series appearances is fifteen years; unless you were born in 1982 and died in 1995, the tragic Donnie Baseball Interregnum, it is physically impossible for you to have "died hard." Besides, you were only fourteen, you little worm.

Clearly, I am handling this Yankee thing rather well.

Yankee dynasties, like Red Sox cataclysms, are probably good for baseball. They remind us that life is not fair, that some are born to sweet delight, some are born to endless night. The Yanks, omnipotent deities, win all the time as they're supposed to win. More power to them. But there's no poetry in their victories. They have a huge checkbook. They open it. But Yankees fans trying to trade old war stories bring to mind the scene in *Cobb,* where the aging Georgia Peach gets refused entrance to a private Cooperstown party filled to overflowing with the lions of the game. Sorry, guys, us ordinary fans from Detroit and Cincinnati are busy discussing blown pennants, false springs, good riddance, bad trades. We don't want you in here. You don't have standing.

IN DISCUSSING THE FAN CANON, ATTENTION MUST BE paid to the spectators' ambivalent relationship with the athletes they pay to see. It is no secret that fans feel disconnected from the players, but tied forever to the game they play. Many, perhaps most, athletes are like high priests who serve a God they do not believe in. The fans care about championships. The athletes care about money. Too often it is forgotten that athletes feel less emotional kinship with their teams than the fans do, because the athletes didn't grow up rooting for the teams they play for. Besides, they get traded. Fans never get traded.

A few sports fans are delusional enough to think that if they were in the professionals' shoes they would play better than the athletes. But most merely believe they would play harder. Sports fans do not identify with supremely gifted athletes like Michael Jordan and Barry Bonds, but they do identify with scrappers like Pete Rose and John Starks. Or, at least, they identify with them until they get caught betting on baseball or missing fifteen of seventeen shots in game 7 of the NBA finals. At this point, fans find somebody else to identify with.

The problem for fans of all stripes is that no matter how good they are at what they do, they will never hit a buzzer-beating jumper or make a game-saving tackle. Sports detractors love to moan about the warped values of a society that pays teachers $25,000 a year but pays men 1,000 times as much to connect with a tiny horsehide spheroid three times out of ten. But lots of people can teach grade school; it takes real talent to hit a tiny spheroid three times out of ten, especially when it is traveling ninety-eight miles an hour and headed straight for your ear. To extend the analogy, anyone can run the Securities and Exchange Commission (Harvey Pitt), anyone can write a novel (Ethan Hawke), anyone can paint a painting (Buddy Ebsen), and anyone can win the Nobel Peace Prize (Yasir Arafat, Jimmy Carter). But try guarding Shaq.

The players, of course, know this. And they have long memories. As Bernard Malamud put it in *The Natural*: "The fans dearly loved Roy but Roy did not love the fans. He hadn't forgotten the dirty treatment they had dished out during the time of his trouble. Often he felt he would like to ram their cheers down their throats." But Malamud gives the fans a chance to get in their two cents; at another point in the book, a woman tells the doomed hero, "I hate to see a hero fail. There are so few of them," adding, "I felt that if you knew people believed in you, you'd regain your power."

It is not entirely clear that the players need the fans' help in this area. The players, of course, are divinities. And like most divinities, they know it. When Frank Sinatra was nearing the end of his career, I asked my mother if she wanted to go see him at Radio City Music Hall. My mother, slightly younger than Sinatra, enthusiastically agreed, but only with the proviso that she could put cotton in her ears throughout Don Rickles' remorselessly crude opening act. After a bland, uninspired set by the Count Basie Ghost Band—Basie and most of his colleagues were long gone—an unseen announcer said, "Ladies and gentlemen, Francis Albert Sinatra."

When the aging, infirm Sinatra ambled out onto the stage, my immediate reaction was a strange sort of disbelief. Sinatra, the first entertainer from my parents' generation that I actually liked, had been as much a part of my childhood as Jackie Gleason, Milton Berle, and Fulton J. Sheen. But it had never occurred to me that he actually existed. It was like seeing Charlemagne or Lawrence of Arabia or Gordon of Khartoum or El Cid. I half-thought the man walking across the stage must be a hologram, that there couldn't be a real Frank Sinatra. It was like the time I visited Mount Vernon and saw a sign directing guests to the tomb of George Washington. Wait a minute, George Washington is actually buried somewhere? I thought he'd been assumed directly into Paradise.

With aging athletes, one often has a similar experience. I saw Willie Mays and Sandy Koufax play when I was a teen, and at the time had no trouble believing in their existence: Koufax always pitched a two-hit shutout with thirteen strikeouts, and Mays always went four for five, with two homers, five RBIs, and the game winner in the top of the eleventh. But I saw them from the cheap seats; they were stick men. Years later, when I saw Willie Mays walking down Park Avenue, I had trouble believing my eyes. It was like standing in front of the *Mona Lisa* for the first time and realizing that while a performance of *Hamlet* or Beethoven's Ninth Symphony was a rendition of a masterpiece, this was the masterpiece itself.

In Mays's case, I could believe that he had once been a center fielder for the San Francisco Giants, that he was, at the time, the oldest man to ever win the MVP award (he was thirty-four in 1965), that he made that breathtaking catch in the 1954 World Series. What I couldn't believe was that he also existed as a creature of flesh and blood, as a man. Mays, the greatest player I ever saw, was a god. The feet of the gods never touched the ground. Yet here he was, right out on Park Avenue.

Of course the god promptly shooed me away when I tried to say hey.

A lesser man might have been permanently scarred by this experience. In point of fact, I *am* a lesser man. But I am not the kind of man who would ever let an experience like this make me rethink my attitude toward athletes, because I long ago decided that the athletes really don't have a whole lot to do with this. There are only about 5,000 of them active at any given time; there are hundreds of millions of fans. Athletes do not grow up applying tourniquets and coughing up blood, living and dying with the teams they play for; they are frequently uninterested in their old clubs, and even their old sports, when they retire. In any case, intelligent fans have always been capable of distinguishing between the player and the man; a good friend from Milwaukee had a similar experience with Lew Alcindor when he was a young boy growing up in Milwaukee and the ex-UCLA great refused to give him an autograph. That didn't make him any less grateful to Alcindor for snaring that lone Bucks championship.

O. J. Simpson provides an even more illuminating example. When O.J. made his break for the border and the network cut away from the Knicks-Rockets final to document his flight, a lot of Americans were outraged. What made a retired football player so important that an entire nation could become obsessed with his plight? I'll tell you what. O. J. Simpson was one of the Immortals. And this was not the first time an entire nation was transfixed by his mad dashes. In the late 1960s when Simpson was a running back at Southern California, the entire country would shut down on Saturday afternoons to watch him play. We were drawn to him like moths to a flame because we *were* moths and O. J. Simpson *was* the flame. O. J. Simpson was the first player in the history of the National Football League to rush for 2,000 yards; he wasn't some bum. We knew this guy. We liked this guy. He had achieved the almost unimaginable feat of being so great—like Michael Jordan, Larry Bird, Julius Erving—that even fans from opposing cities idolized him. How he had come to this savage impasse affected all fans. Because the O. J. Simpson we knew and loved was no longer O. J. Simpson.

Still, what is important here is not Simpson himself but the set of shared emotions that he inspires. Sports is without doubt the most powerful bonding element in the world. Well, at least for males. My father was a fair-weather fan who flitted back and forth from team to team, depending on whether they were winning. But he was an inexhaustible font of mythology. When I was growing up, he would tell me amazing stories about Sugar Ray Robinson drinking blood before his fights, of Joe DiMaggio saluting the flag while catching a fly ball, of ancient hurlers pitching back-to-back complete games punctuated by a few snorts at the bar outside the right-field fence at Connie Mack Stadium. He told me about Ty Cobb sharpening his cleats, Ted Williams refusing to tip his hat to the fans, Babe Ruth calling his shot in Chicago. Manly men being spectacularly manly. Take notes, sonny.

My favorite story concerned Billy Conn, the feisty Irish-American lightweight who bulked up to duke it out with Joe Louis for the heavyweight crown in June 1941 and had the Brown Bomber whipped as the thirteenth round began. Between rounds, so my father said, Conn's trainer told him to stay away from Louis. But Conn wanted the knockout and went after the champ, who floored him with two seconds left in the round. The two boxers had a rematch at Yankee Stadium in 1946, and Louis knocked him out again. Years later, Conn and Louis were at a social event, and Conn said, "Joe, you were heavyweight champion for years; why couldn't you let me be champ for six months?" To which Louis replied, "Billy, you couldn't be heavyweight champion of the world for one round; what makes you think you could have held the title for six months?"

I loved these stories so much that I never bothered to find out if they were true. My father, whatever else his failings, had introduced me to a mysterious past inhabited by titans like Archie Moore, Jack Dempsey, and Rocky Marciano, curiosities like Gorgeous George, tragic figures like Primo Carnera, and dangerous-sounding men with names like Firpo and Graziano. When the time came, I wanted to share those stories with my son, tossing in a few anecdotes about Muhammad Ali, George Foreman, Sugar Ray Leonard, and Smokin' Joe Frazier. Like my father before me, it would be my job to help keep these legends alive. Otherwise, the forgotten players—Three Finger Brown, Sudden Sam McDowell, and yes, even Putsy Caballero—would become like forgotten civilizations: the enigmatic Etruscans, the dimly remembered Hittites, the low-profile Nubians. Being a die-hard sports fan entailed a certain level of responsibility to succeeding generations and homage to previous ones. We were keepers of the flame. We were not doing this simply for fun.

Human life is filled with experiences that seem quite ordinary at the time and only assume a fabled stature with the passage of the years. The little boy out for the day with his father does not know that he will one day be an old man who can walk into a room and dispense the jaw-dropping news that he once saw Babe Ruth and Ty Cobb in the flesh, and deliver it with the same matter-of-factness as saying, "I was with Lee at Antietam." When I saw Willie Mays, Warren Spahn, and Sandy Koufax, I of course knew that they were great players, but I had no way of knowing that they would one day be great old players, that their exploits would be so firmly ensconced in the past that they would assume the stature of Honus Wagner and Grover Cleveland Alexander. What's more, I didn't actually like them when they were playing. Willie Stargell, Gordie Howe, and Bill Russell are among the finest human beings to ever grace this forlorn planet, but when they were playing I hated them. When Bob Gibson and Juan Marichal came to town, I didn't go to Connie Mack Stadium hoping the Phils would win. I went there hoping they would get a hit.

I did not fully realize how quickly the ongoing present becomes the distant past until the day the previously mentioned callow youth traveling from Chicago to New York asked me if I ever saw Reggie Jackson play. Christ Almighty, I fired back, of course I saw Reggie Jackson play. He didn't retire until 1987. But I also saw Roberto Clemente, Hank Aaron, Stan Musial, and Ernie Banks, just as my father saw Joe DiMaggio, Ted Williams, Mickey Mantle, and Robin Roberts. So of course I had seen Reggie Jackson. In fact, I was at the game when Jackson hit his last home run as a Yankee in October 1981. I remember that day vividly, because I was literally watching an era die. It had been Reggie's club; now it was Dave Winfield's team. This was not going to be pleasant. Still, I was somewhat taken aback by the youngster's obvious awe. *Take it easy, kiddo. It's not like I saw Cy Young.*

■ ● ■

BUT LET US RETURN FROM OUR WHIMSICAL REVERIE AND refocus our attention on the anguish and humiliation that is the stock-in-trade, the daily regimen of the ordinary fan. While long-past sporting events always take on an Arthurian hue, contemporary sporting events are brutish, painful, lacking in romance. Looking over our shoulders, we can always see Camelot. Looking straight ahead of us, we usually see Alcatraz. Given the daunting obstacles that confront us—owner greed, player arrogance, coaching incompetence, announcer buffoonery, revolting food, inadequate parking, and the ubiquitous Steinbrennerian shadow—how do fans go on? What do they get out of all this? Could their time be better spent elsewhere? Are fruitful hobbies the answer? Volunteerism? Does any of this have any meaning? Or are we all just clowning around?

This enigma finally sorted itself out for me a couple of years ago when my publisher dispatched me on a cross-country shilling mission. Everywhere I went, it seemed, at least one straw had been placed within easy clutching reach of the fans. The tour started in New York, where the Yankees were limbering up for what they assumed would be their fifth world championship in six years. Then I headed down to Philadelphia, where the 76ers were in the NBA finals and the Phillies, amazingly, had an eight-game lead over the Braves. Moseying on down south, I passed through Baltimore, which had just won the Super Bowl, on my way to Washington, D.C., where Michael Jordan was making noises about coming out of retirement and restoring the cataleptic Wizards to the greatness they had once known as the Bullets.

Out in Minneapolis, the Twins had set the baseball world on its ear by opening a huge lead over the Indians. In Milwaukee, baseball fans had their brand-new, state-of-the-art stadium and were still pumped up about the Bucks' performance in the NBA semifinals, taking the 76ers to seven games. And in Chicago, I had to pay scalpers for tickets to get into Wrigley, with the Cubs four games out in front. Later that year, the Bears would surprise everyone by going 13–3.

On the West Coast, the euphoria continued. Seattle fans were watching their record-setting Mariners run away with the American League West title. A few miles to the south, I arrived in Portland the very day that Maurice Cheeks was named head coach of the talented but dysfunctional Trail Blazers team, who should have won the NBA championship the previous year. In San Francisco, fans were all abuzz about Barry Bonds's assault on Mark McGwire's home run mark, and by the time I arrived in Los Angeles, the Lakers had won their second consecutive NBA championship.

My travels did not take me to Denver (Avalanche wins the Stanley Cup), Detroit (Red Wings dynasty still intact), Cleveland (home of the perennial pennant-contending Indians), or Boston (Patriots win the Super Bowl). But you get the general idea. It is all an amazing shell game. Everywhere you go, provided you don't arrive during the last week of the season, the fans are on a semipermanent high. There is always a spanking-new stadium, a budding superstar, a stunning trade, a fat-cat owner, a brash new coach. The powers-that-be have rigged the whole deal by creating so many divisions and so many playoffs that every major city has something to get excited about. In Dallas, the Cowboys were abysmal, but the hockey team had recently won the Stanley Cup and the Rangers had just acquired Alex Rodriguez. In Houston, the Astros were making a serious run at the National League flag. And Phoenix, loaded for bear with Phillies exile Curt Schilling and Mariners castoff Randy Johnson, was on its way to winning the World Series. Today is always the first day in the rest of the average fan's life. No matter how many times the fans see the magic trick, they retain the miraculous ability to be shocked and amazed by the reemergence of the same old rabbit.

JOURNALISTS AND SPORTSCASTERS ARE FOREVER OBSESSing about the gallant Boys of Summer or the predatory Michael Jordan or the legendarily bumbling New York Mets of the early 1960s, because it is easy to write about the obviously great or the obviously horrible. But this is not the way fans view the games. Fans view the games through a municipal rather than a mythological prism; everything is tied in with where you grew up, whom your dad rooted for, how many times your team has broken your heart. That's why I did not read Kahn's book until last summer. The book is about a team that played in Brooklyn that usually won the pennant. My team played in Philly and usually lost the pennant. All things considered, I'd rather be in Philadelphia. Reading about the Ice Capades.

But such an attitude is foolish and crass. We *are* all in this together. Well, most of us. Without being able to commiserate with disappointed sports fans from other cities or to take pleasure in the good fortune of others, the fan would wind up a shriveled old prune, an outcast at life's rich feast.

When I was twenty-two, I took a bus trip across the heartland of America. I particularly recall a Sunday morning I spent riding with a bunch of chirpy St. Louis Cardinals fans who were on their way to Busch Stadium. Generally speaking, I hate Cardinals fans, because their team stole the 1964 pennant from its rightful owners. But these people got on the bus in Tulsa, Oklahoma. At seven o'clock in the morning.

You had to be impressed.

Once, while visiting Pittsburgh, I asked a Steel City native if he could show me the site of Forbes Field, which had been torn down in 1971. He did. What I did not know until we pulled up at midnight was that the wall over which Bill Mazeroski belted his Series-wining home run in 1960 was still standing, though the rest of the stadium had been razed. I had grown up hating the Pirates—large, mean cats playing with Philadelphia's eensy-meansy mice—but as I stood at the foot of the wall with my son as the witching hour tolled, I could practically feel tears in my eyes.

"Do the Yankees ever play in Pittsburgh?" I asked him.

"Not since Mazeroski hit that home run," he replied. "They're afraid to come back."

You had to be impressed.

That said, it would be remiss to overlook the Manichaean nature of the true fan's relationship to his teams. By this I mean that, while one is morally obligated to root, root, root for the home team, it is also perfectly acceptable to maintain a simultaneous hatred of the franchise and to curse the moment it first saw the light of day. I personally believe that the Eagles and the Phillies have each taken about five years off my life through their vaudevillian antics down through the decades. As a friend once put it, the difference between the Phillies and the Third Reich is that after the Second World War, a few of the Nazis apologized for their crimes against humanity, while the boys in the colorful red pinstripes have remained obstreperously mute on this subject.

In the late Clinton administration, when belated and ultimately meaningless national apologies—to American Indians, to African-Americans, to Bosnians (oh yes, the Vatican also got into the act with a tearful apology to Jews for 2,000 years of uninterrupted Christian villainy)—became all the rage, I anxiously awaited the moment when the Phillies' owners would apologize for the infamous 1964 meltdown, which, as I've perhaps already mentioned, ruined my life. But the apology never came. The truth is, I would have been happy if Clinton himself had adopted a surrogate's role and apologized to the people of Philadelphia on the part of the team's craven, unrepentant owners. But that apology never came, either. (On a personal note, I do not actually recall any Nazis apologizing for their crimes against humanity, and I am certain that if they did apologize, it was only to escape hanging. Still, I understand my friend's feelings on the matter. He was there in 1964, too.)

Acrimony so intense, so uncompromising, so vicious, so unhealthy underscores the one tenet of the fan canon that is absolutely biblical in its inflexibility: *Never forgive, never forget.* Stated simply, a man who does not know how to hate can never truly learn to love. When the films *North Dallas Forty* and *Semi-Tough* were first released, I went to see them not because I particularly cared for the work of the Messieurs Nolte and Reynolds but because the teams that ended up on the losing end in those films came from Dallas. For my entire adult life, whenever people ask me why I hate the Cowboys so much, I have always said it was because Dallas killed my president. But the honest truth is, I hate the team because defensive back Mike Gechter once clotheslined Eagles running back Timmy Brown toward the end of his career in a completely meaningless game whose outcome was no longer in doubt.

Last year I found out that it was Leroy Jordan who clotheslined Timmy Brown.

I still hate Gechter.

3

FANS WHO RUN IN FRONT

AT PRECISELY 9:07 A.M. ON APRIL 2, 1985, THE MORNING after the Villanova Wildcats pulled off the biggest upset in NCAA history, I was walking across Times Square when I happened to spot a preening jackass wearing a spanking-new Villanova Wildcats bomber jacket. Since nobody in New York actually likes the Villanova Wildcats—it was then and is now a hard-core St. John's town—and since it was evident to the naked eye that the man was hardly college material, I realized that I was in the presence of one of the most adept, turn-on-a-dime front-runners in history.

To all appearances, this Johnny-come-lately had waited until the Wildcats had polished off the heavily favored Georgetown Hoyas, captained by *überunterperformer* Patrick Ewing, then slept outside the now defunct Hermann's sporting goods store, waiting to be the first person in Gotham to don the sort of geographically incongruous attire that would enable him to sneer, "I told you so."

Recognizing that I would one day take pen in hand and geld the ostentatious weasel, but still willing to give him the benefit of the doubt (as any good, fair-minded journalist would), I asked where he was from, what connection he had with Villanova University, who Howard Porter was, and how long he had been a Wildcats fan. The answers were: Queens, none, no idea, and "as long as I can remember." Howard Porter, far and away the greatest player in Wildcat history, anchored the 1971 team that lost the NCAA championship to UCLA. The Wildcats' second-place finish was later expunged from the official record because Porter, who played seven so-so years in the NBA, had already signed a contract with an agent. In other words, this scoundrel had been a Villanova fan since about 11:32 the previous evening. I knew these things because I graduated from St. Joseph's College, the despised crosstown rivals of the tony, upscale Wildcats, and even though I was happy to see Villanova win the title, since the prissy, suburban school has some vague connection to the City of Brotherly Love, I still despised the place. But I also knew it because I had been following college basketball since 1964.

The incident was much in my thoughts at Christmas three years ago when my son and I went gift shopping for my nephew Frank, who lives in Harrisburg, Pennsylvania. Culturally marooned between his hometown of Philadelphia, which he fled as a small child, and the Steel City, much farther to the west, and raised by his mother, who is not an avid sports fan, Frank grew up with a fractured sense of franchisal fidelity.

A product of the don't-pin-me-down, I-root-for-anybody-who's-hot *Sports Center* generation, Frank grew up with team affiliations that were literally all over the lot. In the early 1990s, while still a teen, he suddenly took a shine to the Cincinnati Reds, surprise winners of the 1991 World Series. At roughly the same time, he welcomed the Los Angeles Lakers aboard the Good Ship *Fairweather.* Over the past decade or so he has fleetingly set his cap for the Oakland Athletics (who won the World Series in 1990) and the New York Mets (who never won the World Series in the 1990s, but who always acted like they had), and has throughout his short lifetime repeatedly provided incontrovertible proof of his latest improvised emotional liaisons by purchasing official team haberdashery.

Frank's ice hockey passions have carried him all the way to the swamps of the miasmic northern Jersey swamplands, where his enthusiasm for the mesmerizingly uninteresting New Jersey Devils coincided with the first of that mysterious franchise's two Stanley Cups. And last but not least, he became an enthusiastic Indianapolis Colts fan shortly after Peyton Manning was drafted first in the 1998 NFL draft.

To recapitulate the inventory: Cincy, L.A., Queens, Jersey, the Hoosier State. I do not do my nephew an injustice by stating that as a fan, his pudding has no theme.

Which is why my son, Gordon, and I went Christmas shopping. Concerned that Frank was in danger of falling into the sunshine patriot's abyss, my son and I purchased a Yankees T-shirt, a Devils wristband, a St. Louis Rams watch cap, and a leather Los Angeles Lakers gimme cap, wrapped them up nicely, and shipped them out to Harrisburg. All these teams had just won their respective championships, so when Frank opened the package on Christmas morning, the message was clear: he had been kitted out with a complete new wardrobe from the House of Front-running. My son and I even took the extra step of picking out a Yankees T-shirt with the name Mussina on the back; as the money-grubbing Orioles fugitive had not yet pitched a single inning for the Bronx Bombers, this gave my nephew a chance to participate in an increasingly popular phenomenon known as *preemptive front-running*.

Frank was miffed by the poorly camouflaged subtext implied by this lurid ensemble, insisting that he was a rabid Colts fan and had worshiped the Devils from afar since he was knee-high to a grasshopper. I was ready to accept him at his word, but as I had explained on innumerable occasions, his philosophy of fan fealty was geographically unacceptable. A person who had been born in the City of Brotherly Love was morally obligated to root for the Phillies, the Eagles, the 76ers, and the Flyers throughout his life, and this support must be unconditional. Any other road led straight to perdition.

Given that my nephew had moved to central Pennsylvania while still a young boy, and thus was in no way responsible for his mother's decision to seek a better life on the banks of the mighty Susquehanna, I was prepared to confer my grudging seal of approval if he transferred his allegiances to the teams from Pittsburgh, even though the Steel City is 205 miles from Harrisburg, whereas Philadelphia is a scant 107. A strong case could be made for doing so. In the early 1990s, the Penguins won two consecutive Stanley Cups under the inspired leadership of Mario Lemieux, who had recovered from Hodgkin's disease, and contended for numerous others. Twice the Bonds-Bonilla Buckos came within an eyelash of the World Series, each time succumbing to the Atlanta Braves. And the Steelers played the Cowboys in Super Bowl XXX, a game they would have won had Neil O'Donnell not gift-wrapped two interceptions to the otherwise useless Larry Brown. (Brown played a couple of pointless years with the Oakland Raiders; O'Donnell went on to lead the New York Jets to several malodorous seasons.) Meanwhile, the Philly teams basically stunk.

The point of all this was simple: Fan support must be based on one of two criteria. Either you grew up in a specific locality and inherited a congenital municipal connection to the team, or you grew up somewhere else but rooted for your father's teams. (In certain rare instances an exception could be made for supporting a team simply because your uncle Sal did. But only if he was really your uncle Sal and not some mythical figure you dreamed up to make your perfidy seem more palatable to your naive, gullible friends.)

On the other hand, it was morally unacceptable, an outrage against the law of God and man, to root for teams with which these emotional or geographic ties did not exist. For starters, it weakened our national moral character by promulgating the notion that it was permissible to arbitrarily switch allegiances. Such deviations from the unwritten laws of the universe led inevitably to such outrages as the Rosenbergs, Tokyo Rose, Benedict Arnold, and John Walker Lindh. It was one of God's few serious oversights; He should have excised the redundant "Thou Shalt Not Covet Thy Neighbor's Goods" from the Ten Commandments ("Thou Shalt Not Steal" pretty well covers it) and inserted "Thou Shalt Not Run in Front" instead. And then He wonders why so many Vikings fans take His name in vain.

Am I exaggerating here? I most certainly am not. A nation that encourages its citizens to cavalierly switch allegiances breeds a moral ambivalence and general spinelessness that will ultimately lead to the collapse of the Republic. A man who could root for the Bulls one year and for the Lakers the next is the kind of man who could easily throw in his lot with the Reds (no, not the ones from Cincinnati), the Nazis, the Taliban, Shining Path, and yes, perhaps even the feared Druze militiamen. I am certain that if historians set their minds to it, they would effortlessly unearth damning evidence that Pétain, Quisling, and that treacherous Greek goatherd who revealed the hidden path to the invading Persians at the Battle of Thermophylae were all front-runners. But historians always have better things to do.

Yet the evidence is there. We need look no farther than Judas Iscariot, who, by switching allegiances from Jesus Christ to Pontius Pilate, revealed himself to be the most abhorrent front-runner of all time. But at least Judas got thirty pieces of silver for his efforts. Front-running Magic fans get nothing.

I cannot overestimate how strongly I feel about this issue. In March 2002 I visited the hallowed battlefield of Culloden, which sits on a hill about two miles outside the picturesque northern Scottish city of Inverness. It was in the marshes of Culloden on April 16, 1746, that Bonnie Prince Charlie was defeated by the duke of Cumberland, thus permanently smashing tenuous dreams of Scottish independence and/or planting a Roman Catholic on the throne of England. While it is true that Bonnie Prince Charlie was a classic Franco-Caledonian knucklehead, a first-class bozo in a second-class society, and that his initially fruitful invasion of England itself was an ill-conceived undertaking from the start, it is also true that he was defeated at Culloden by an invading army that included a substantial number of Scots. You can find descendants of these McChurls at every Super Bowl, every World Series, every NCAA Final Four. They're the ones who wait until one team is incontrovertibly assured of victory before deciding which side to root for. I went to Culloden with the specific mission of spitting on their ancestors' graves. I am nothing if not vindictive.

AT THIS POINT, IT MIGHT BE USEFUL TO INVESTIGATE THE very nature of front-running. Although we tend to think of front-runners as flighty, morally malleable types who expeditiously jump on the closest bandwagon whenever a team is poised for victory, front-running is actually an extremely complex activity replete with myriad variations. Front-runners, like necrophiliacs and patricides, share certain characteristics, yet to arbitrarily lump them all in the same category betrays an appalling disregard for methodological subtlety and epidemiological nuance.

Front-running in its most obvious form is the sort practiced by movie stars and related celebrities who never fail to show up at courtside once a team—any team—is on the verge of winning a championship. Generally speaking, this activity is associated with the Los Angeles Lakers and the New York Yankees, because there are no celebrities in places like Cleveland and Portland. But should the New Orleans Saints ever battle their way into the Super Bowl, TV viewers would no doubt be treated to zoom shots of sidelines jam-packed with shopworn celebrities sporting brand-new Archie Manning jerseys, who would be on the next plane back to Tinseltown should the Saints go into the tank. As they invariably do.

A variation of celebrity front-running is the kind witnessed throughout the 1990s during the Pat Reilly/Patrick Ewing mini-epoch at Madison Square Garden. Here celebrities of all hues and stature—*Hey! Who gave Matthew Modine a ticket?*—would turn up at the games simply to get their cadaverous mugs on the national feed in the hope of reviving their sagging careers. Although the Knicks never won the NBA championship, they got to the finals twice and were bounced in the semifinals on numerous other occasions. They were like Hannibal's Carthaginians to Scipio Africanus's Romans: flashy and self-involved, but incapable of winning the big one because they had too many lumbering elephants on the squad.

Since the Knicks were invariably dispatched by the Bulls back in this era, celebrities got to kill two birds with one stone: simultaneously basking in the reflected aura of both Michael Jordan and Pat Reilly, without revealing their true passions until the last second. We refer to this phenomenon as *luminary fence-sitting* or *bifurcative front-running*. (Knicks front-runners who jumped ship as soon as Ewing & Co. were bounced from the regional finals are also sometimes referred to as *divisional front-runners,* the *regionally untrustworthy,* or *early-round Iagos.*)

Bicoastal front-running is a genre that boasts only a few practitioners, yet because it is unspeakably malevolent, it bears comment here. NBA fans will recall that in the flashy "Showtime" Lakers era back in the 1980s the erstwhile Knicks fan John McEnroe was frequently seen at courtside in Los Angeles rooting for Magic Johnson and the gang. Then, when the collapse of his marriage fortuitously coincided with the rise of the Knicks and the decline of the Lakers, he returned to courtside at Madison Square Garden and rooted for the hometown Knicks, whom he presumably grew up worshiping in Queens, though for all I know he may have been a New York Nets fan back in the days when Julius Erving was winning two American Basketball Association titles. McEnroe would probably like us to believe that he rooted for the Lakers for a short period not because he had gone Hollywood but because he was temporarily living on the West Coast. But deep down inside his heart was not really in it. It was all a charade.

Mr. McEnroe, *you cannot be serious.*

We can now proceed to the more relevant topic of *mainstream front-running,* as practiced by millions of loathsome scabs, feckless scoundrels, pasty-faced mongrels, and unindicted curs. The prototypical fair-weather fan is the individual who consistently roots for a certain team or a group of teams, but only roots for them when they are winning. "I just couldn't watch the Mets in the early nineties because they were so bad" is how one of my friends puts it. *O, thou scabrous reptile, thou cream-faced loon, thou pussy toad.* Here we come eyeball to eyeball with the core emotional deficiency in the front-runner's psyche: his failure to comprehend that the thrill of victory is made a million times sweeter by the memory of defeat. As the doomed Debra Winger explains it to Anthony Hopkins when the Grim Reaper puts in an appearance toward the end of *Shadowlands*, "The happiness then is part of the pain now. And that's the deal."

Was she talking about the Buffalo Bills, circa 1990–93? Probably not. But the point is well taken. The fan who does not support his team through thick and thin, come what may, gamely clinging to his cause through the dark night of the soul, can never truly participate in the rapture of victory. What's more, he has no right to participate in that victory.

Or so it is said by the wise ones in the hills.

The compulsive front-runner is the type of fair-weather fan who shifts allegiances at the drop of a hat. *I used to be a Phillies fan, but now I am an Athletic supporter.* Step into his closet and you will find any number of Duke Blue Devils, Chicago Bulls, and San Francisco 49ers jackets, caps, and wristbands. He is the type of fan who is incapable of supporting any team that is unlikely to win the next championship because he believes it reflects badly on him as a person. This is a juvenile mind-set, because it is foolish for these people to worry about things reflecting badly on them. Everything reflects badly on them. They are very bad people.

The *incoherent front-runner* is the type of person who supports both the Knicks and the Bulls, the Lakers and the Celtics, the Fighting Irish and the Miami Hurricanes, without being aware that part of the moral responsibility of rooting for these teams is to hate their rivals and pray for their destruction. Cheering for both sides is like being a steak lover *and* a vegetarian.

The *anachronistic front-runner* is the kind of fan who boldly asserts his liberal credentials by proudly sporting the colors of Negro League teams whose legendary players never got to play in the big leagues. By wearing a Kansas City Monarchs or a Pittsburgh Crawfords cap, the anachronistic front-runner asserts that had he been alive at the time such injustices were visited on Josh Gibson and Satchel Paige, he would have sacrificed everything, even his life, to ensure that the color line was crossed and the ramparts of racial inequity were torn down. Yeah. Sure.

Other varieties of front-running can be quickly dispatched. *Reflexive, knee-jerk front-running* is the type exhibited by suits. *We only root for teams that win because supporting teams that lose would make us look like, well, losers.* (For further reading, consult "Clinton, Hillary: Overnight Affection for Yankees While Running for the U.S. Senate.") *Serial front-runners* switch allegiances every season. *Tautological front-runners* wait until game 5 of the Subway Series to decide whether they are Yankees or Mets fans, because they love all things New York. This, of course, flies in the face of reality, since the sworn mission of all Mets fans—defined in the cradle—is to despise the Yankees, because they always buy their championships, and the mission of all Yankees fans is to ignore the Mets, because they always try to buy a championship and always come up a bit short. Rooting for both the Mets and the Yankees is like rooting for both the IRA and the Black and Tans. Make up your mind, you repellent ding-dong.

Next up are *ethnic front-runners;* that is, shameless African-Americans who start out rooting for the Bulls, then abruptly switch to the Magic, and then finally pin their hopes on the Lakers because they claim an intimate ethnic liaison with Michael Jordan, Shaquille O'Neal, Penny Hardaway, Kobe Bryant, and then Shaquille O'Neal again. In their diseased minds, they think that being black gives them a free pass to be disloyal to the home teams in Cleveland, Houston, Denver, et cetera. Since the Atlanta Hawks also have a preponderance of black players on the squad, this squalid ethnic card will not work. If you're a chrome-domed black Bostonian who roots for the Chicago Bulls, you're just as bad as the tattooed mullethead from St. Louis who roots for the Detroit Red Wings. You're still a snake in the grass, and God will one day bring down the hammer on your sorry ass.

One of the most loathsome forms of front-running is *xenoparvenuism,* the kind practiced by foreigners. On a visit to Limerick, Ireland, a few years ago, I briefly conversed with a man who was an avid Manchester United football fan. Manchester is the fabulously wealthy British team that always buys the best players and wins championships by the fistful. Manchester, when last I looked, is located in central England; Limerick, when last I checked, is in central Ireland. I wasn't terribly surprised when this Finian front-runner divulged that he was also a Yankees fan but had rooted for the Toronto Blue Jays against the Phillies in 1993; it fit the M.O. Bear in mind that the Irish remained neutral during the Second World War, and that the first president of the Irish Free State personally ordered the murder of his closest friend, the fearless Michael Collins, without whose efforts there would not even be an Irish Republic. If you were looking for people ready to switch allegiances at the drop of a hat, you had come to the right place.

The *fugitive front-runner* is the type of fan who switches allegiances so regularly and with such bewildering speed that his friends and neighbors never get a chance to taunt him when his team loses. Part of being a sports fan, and a large part of being a fan, consists of wearing your team's colors and visibly proclaiming your allegiances. This entitles you to preen and gloat when your team wins, but it also confers the responsibility of cursing, swearing, wrecking your car, and just falling into a general funk for months after your team loses. The fugitive front-runner eludes such misfortune by immediately burning his sports merchandise as soon as his team loses and then announcing, "I stopped rooting for those bums years ago."

Transmunicipal front-running is an activity practiced in towns that field competing franchises in the same sport. I have found little evidence of it in Los Angeles, where historically there has rarely been any reason to switch affections from the Dodgers to the Angels, or in Chicago, where an entrenched North Side–South Side cultural divide exists. But in New York it happens all the time, most recently when thousands of lifelong Rangers fans defected to the Devils. The North Jersey *franchisette* is more than happy to greet these untrustworthy vermin, because the Devils do not have a scientifically verifiable fan base. The Devils, like the Los Angeles Clippers, are tangential teams who owe their existence to the fact that they play in markets large enough to support a substantial TV audience even though they have almost no dyed-in-the-wool adherents. When the Devils won their first Stanley Cup in 1995, the red-faced management was forced to hold the victory parade in the parking lot because the franchise does not have a core constituency or a municipality to which it is connected. They might as well play on Uranus or Mars; they'd certainly draw better.

The *retroactive front-runner,* another sublimely repellent type, always insists that his support of a team dates back generations. This pernicious specimen, commonly seen at ticker-tape parades, can immediately be identified by his brand-new Los Angeles Lakers cap, by his astonished gaze when told that the team he now supports once played in Milwaukee and Boston, and by the fact that he does not know that Yankee Stadium is located in the Bronx. When the Green Bay Packers suddenly crawl out of the crypt after a quarter century of impotence and disgrace, faux Favre fans in sports bars from Waukegan to Santa Fe instantaneously slap on those hideous green-and-gold costumes—which only look good on football players—and pretend they were fervent Packer fans all through the long dark decades in the Cheesehead Wilderness. Attention, Wisconsin death squads: When confronted by one of these perfidious oafs, ask him what Dan Devine's won-loss record was. Watch the cur stutter and gag. Then behead him.

Of course, the *cordon bleu* of retroactive front-runners is the unregenerate cad who insists that he was present at one of the epochal events in his team's history. When the Green Bay Packers defeated the Dallas Cowboys in the legendary "Ice Bowl," on December 31, 1967, a day so cold one of the officials had to referee the game with a whistle stuck to his lips, there were 50,861 fans in attendance. By now, their numbers have swelled to 1.5 million. This is roughly the same number that claim to have seen Wilt Chamberlain score 100 points at Madison Square Garden or Convention Hall in Philadelphia on March 2, 1962. In reality, the game was played in Hershey, Pennsylvania, in front of 4,124 fans. And Wilt was playing for the Philadelphia Warriors, not the 76ers.

SOME READERS MAY ARGUE THAT I AM MAKING TOO MUCH of this front-running business. I have heard their arguments many times before. Why should a young man just starting out as a sports fan automatically be hamstrung by municipal or regional ties? What's wrong with consistently rooting for the team that looks like it has the best chance to win? What's wrong with repackaging one's past, so as to make it appear that one has passionately supported the Jets since the Joe Namath era, that one's affection for the Cleveland Indians goes all the way back to the days of Rocky Colavito and Bob Feller, that one's unwavering passion for the Yankees stems from a leisurely day spent playing hookey in the South Bronx back in the third grade? What's the harm in it all?

Let me answer these questions in order of importance.

1. *Front-runners make a bad situation worse.* One of the only things that make life bearable is the knowledge that we're all in the same lifeboat and the lifeboat is leaking. By deliberately seceding from the municipal lifeboat, the front-runner sets himself apart from the community and refuses to share in their suffering. Such anguish builds character, but more to the point, it cuts across ethnic, racial, political, and economic lines. It enables investment bankers to

communicate amiably with garbagemen, and white people to chat with Spike Lee.

2. *Front-runners do not share.* By virtue of the fact that they do not groan when their companions mention disastrous No. 1 draft picks (Shalor Halimon, Ki-Jana Carter, Ralph Sampson, the Boz), front-runners cannot fully participate in the shared mythology of the tribe to which they seek entrance. They are interlopers, arrivistes, carpetbaggers. At a crucial moment, when the sports fan thinks he cannot bear any more misfortune, they will always say something horrible like, "Come on, guys; it's only a game" or "Well, at least this way we can beat traffic" or "I never really liked the Vikings anyway."
3. *Front-runners refuse to take their medicine.* When things are going badly, these impostors are nowhere to be found; only when the local team wins does the bogus fan want to share and share alike. He is like a peasant living in a doomed village in the Dark Ages who refuses to bond with his fellow man. "I don't care how many of your children have been swept away by bubonic plague," he cackles. "Personally, I have always rooted for the rats."
4. *Front-runners cannot be trusted when the chips are down.* Here it is necessary to choose my words carefully, and I shall. While I will defend to the death the right of a person living in Dallas to root for the suddenly successful Atlanta Braves, and while I do not deny the constitutional right of a person who grew up in Oregon to root for the Crimson Tide, I do not believe that such individuals should ever be married, befriended, employed, feted, consulted, or fed,

> and I certainly do not believe that they should ever be given a ranking position in the State Department or the Nuclear Regulatory Commission. A Rambling Wreck from Georgia Tech who would root for the LSU Tigers or a Roman Catholic who would root against Notre Dame are the kinds of people who would willingly sell vital national secrets to our enemies for thirty pieces of silver. Maybe twenty. Ten in a pinch. Attention, marriageable females: If you go through your Los Angelino boyfriend's closet and find a Chicago Bulls jersey, call off the wedding. If he betrayed the Lakers, he will have no trouble betraying you.

How seriously do I take this subject? I have a notebook containing the names of everyone I know from Philadelphia. I know exactly where they grew up, and I know exactly which teams they have rooted for. When the next championship comes to a Philadelphia team, and these turncoat marsupials try to jump on the bandwagon, I shall make a personal effort to cover them with contumely and expose them as the front-running lickspittles they are. When they die, I will personally pay for headstones that read:

PAT MCGINTY
Born: Philadelphia, November 1, 1950
Died: Dallas, May 1, 2008
Rooted for
New York Yankees (1977–78, 1996, 1998, 1999, 2000)
Boston Celtics (1956–66)
Los Angeles Lakers (1972, 1980, 1982, 1985, 1987, 1988, 2000, 2001, 2002)

Montreal Canadiens (1976–80)
San Francisco 49ers (1982, 1985, 1989, 1990, 1995)
Died as he lived: a stinking front-runner.

As banning the practice of front-running necessarily condemns tens of millions of fans to a lifetime of supporting teams that rarely or never win, isn't this making the future bleak for anyone unlucky enough to be born near Wrigley Field or Fenway? Yes and no. It is true that in its most basic form, the guiding philosophy of the true sports fan must be: Don't do the crime if you can't do the time. Put another way: if you are not prepared to suffer, why the hell did you bother to get born in Buffalo?

Still, there are enormous emotional compensations to be derived from eschewing the front-running arts. For one, defeat prepares you for death, and perhaps even makes it something to look forward to. Second, because your teams win so infrequently, you can effortlessly recall every last detail of the most recent championship run. Front-runners can't do this; they've won so many championships that they can't keep things straight. Moreover, they get inordinately upset on the odd occasions when they don't win; they're like lab rats addicted to the pleasure bar, demon masturbators who will literally stimulate themselves to death. Shortly before Steinbrenner's Hessians took the pipe in October 2002, my local paper carried a photograph of a middle-aged woman holding up a banner that read: THE YANKEES DESERVE ANOTHER WORLD SERIES TITLE.

What, twenty-six wasn't enough?

Or maybe she just hates even numbers.

■ ● ■

GIVEN MY ALMOST PSYCHOPATHIC AVERSION TO FAIR-weather fans and those who book passage on the most proximate bandwagon, a question that presents itself at this point is whether I myself ever succumbed to the siren song of front-runnery. The answer, though it grieves me to admit it, is yes. For a brief period in the late 1960s, without ever forswearing my allegiance to the Philadelphia Eagles, I secretly dabbled in the front-running arts, discreetly morphing into a closet fan of the Baltimore Colts, now relocated to Indianapolis. (As the old saying goes, the sins of the uncle are visited upon the nephew; he who lies down with the Crabcake shall rise up with the Hoosier.) The experience was ultimately tragic and punitive, and forever cured me of a desire to switch allegiances.

The circumstances were these: in the middle 1960s, the Eagles, as is their wont, made one of their intermittent visits to the deepest pit of hell. With no one to root for, I decided to "adopt" the Colts as my second team. The Colts at the time fielded some of the strongest squads of the era, and as they were led by the spindly but charismatic Johnny Unitas, they were lots of fun to watch. But my fleeting support of the team ultimately led to emotional devastation. In 1965, they lost a heartbreaking overtime playoff game to the Packers. In 1966, they drifted. Then, in 1967, the Colts were 11–0–2 going into the last game of the season. If they won their final game against the Rams, whom they had beaten earlier in the season, they would almost certainly represent the NFL in the Super

Bowl and almost certainly triumph. This was not anywhere near as good as having the Eagles win it all, but it was better than nothing. I was an impressionable tyke who had been too young to appreciate the Eagles' upset victory over the Green Bay Packers in the 1960 NFL championship game. With the Eagles destined for a decade and a half of incompetence and disgrace, I was grabbing for a lifeline. Johnny U and the boys from Crabcake Corners provided it.

Tragically, the Colts lost the final game of the season and were eliminated from contention. In 1969 the Colts came back with an even better squad, one of the most potent offensive teams of all time. Easily dispatching the upstart Minnesota Vikings in the NFC championship game, they were tabbed eighteen to twenty-one–point favorites in Super Bowl III. Everyone knows what happened: they suffered a humiliating 16–7 defeat, a mockery of the game so devastating to the NFL powers-that-be that it led to the merger of the two leagues one year later. Although the Colts would win the lackluster Super Bowl V, the first title game featuring the now fused leagues, I had long since stopped rooting for them. They had repeatedly broken my heart, even though they were only my backup team. I hated them.

When I think back on my misguided duplicity of the late 1960s, two thoughts come to mind. First, by shifting allegiances to another team, I had simply opened the floodgates of horror, exposing myself to misfortunes of which the Eagles would have never been capable. (They never lost the big game because they never played any big games.) This taught me an invaluable lesson: Stick with the devil you know rather than the devil that plays in Baltimore. Second, if you're going to be a front-runner, be an effective front-runner. Had I rooted for the Packers rather than the Colts, I would have been treated to two Super Bowl championships, a dynasty, and priceless emotional identification with the immortal Vince Lombardi. More important, I would have been spared the psychological devastation of rooting for the team that became the biggest flop in Super Bowl history. In my malleable, unformed teenage mind, I had somehow persuaded myself that rooting for the Colts made me a bit of a maverick, whereas rooting for the Green Bay Packers would have tarred me as a generic, standard-issue front-runner. I had experimented with a type of front-running that had a limited geographic justification, whereas rooting for the Packers would have made me a complete and utter schmuck. To this day, decades later, I have never seen the team I support win the Super Bowl. All things considered, maybe I should have been a schmuck.

Naturally, these painful memories were revived immediately after the 1998 NFL draft when my nephew suddenly announced that he was, without any further ado, becoming a Colts fan. Like me, Frank had chosen to support a team seemingly headed for numerous Super Bowl championships that then went out and choked. Had my nephew merely done the geographically acceptable thing and rooted for a team from the state he grew up in, he would have been able to bask in the aura of a Super Bowl. True, the Steelers lost the game because of Neil O'Donnell's remarkable incompetence. But the Colts haven't been in the Super Bowl since 1971.

Nonetheless, there is still a faint sliver of hope on the horizon, the fleeting specter of redemption. Several years ago, Frank began attending football games at Penn State, his alma mater. One of the great football powers of the past thirty-five years, the Nittany Lions had recently tumbled into a morass of terrifying medicority. Yet Frank has been unwavering in his support. True, he was probably attracted to the team because the legendary but now inept Joe Paterno was within a few games of the record for most coaching wins. This does not change the fact that Frank has continued to support them through the darkest of dark times. Yes, he betrayed the Phillies, stabbed the Eagles in the back, sneered at the sacred orange and black of the Flyers, and committed the unforgivable sin of cheering on the Lakers during their 2001 championship bout with the feisty 76ers. Adding insult to injury, he has stubbornly refused to root for the noble teams that ply their trade at the junction of the mighty Ohio, the poignant Allegheny and the functional Monongahela. But at least he has found one team to stick with through thick and thin, one team with which he can claim a clear emotional, biographical, and geographic link. At least he has not spat in the face of Joe Paterno. At least he's finally drawn a line in the sand. And for that we can all take small comfort. He may yet change his mind about the Eagles and Phillies. He may yet get a few bucks when my will is read.

4

FANS WHO SEE GREEN

IT IS WIDELY BELIEVED BY PROTESTANTS, AGNOSTICS, SECular humanists, and snake worshipers that all newborn Irish-American males, while still in a highly suggestible state of postobstetric trauma, are taken directly from the delivery room and swaddled in blankets and bonnets festooned with leprechauns, shamrocks, and other images intimately associated with the University of Notre Dame's Fighting Irish football team. This is not true, any more than it is true that all Irish-Americans enjoy *Riverdance*.

What is true is that at an early point in every Irish-American boy's life he is introduced by his father, grandfather, brothers, cousins, or entire ethnic group to the daunting mythology of the Fighting Irish—the Golden Dome, the Golden

Boy, the Four Horsemen, Knute Rockne—and is asked if he would like to spend the rest of his life rooting for Joe Montana's team, which never stumbles, and never falls, or if he would feel more comfortable hitching his star to, say, a Holy Cross or a Villanova.

Not every Irish-American boy succumbs to the siren song of the Fighting Irish. Some strike out on their own paths and grow up to support teams with fierce badgers or feisty mountain lions as mascots. Some even loudly proclaim that they despise Notre Dame, with its padded schedule, inflated scores, haughty alumni, belligerent leprechauns. Many of these iconoclastic individuals go on to lead rich, full lives, becoming captains of industry, respected civic leaders, doting parents. But before the sands of time have trickled through their fingers, all of these ethnic Iscariots meet horrible, celestially engineered fates, just as surely as depraved pop stars who sport crucifixes in otherwise satanic music videos. For being Irish-American and not wanting Notre Dame to win one for the Gipper is like being English and not wanting the RAF to beat the Luftwaffe. It puts one in a culturally untenable position. It makes people suspicious of one's true ethnic background. And it ensures that one will spend all eternity in the deepest, dankest pit of hell. My son, age sixteen, knows this only too well. At birth, he was swaddled in shamrocks, harps, and leprechauns, laid in a manger, and rocked to sleep by Sinead, Clannad, and Altan. And he's half English.

I started rooting for Notre Dame in 1964, the year they blew a 17–0 halftime lead and lost 20–17 to Southern Cal. I was fourteen at the time, and I was devastated. I didn't stay devastated for long; in 1966, the Fighting Irish won the national championship, as they would in 1973, 1977, and 1988. Nineteen sixty-six was the year of the glorious Celtic quarterback tandem (Terry Hanratty to Jim Seymour, with Coley O'Brien in the wings), the year Ara Parseghian elected to play for a tie against Michigan State because he knew the Irish could nail down the No. 1 spot by flaying Southern Cal 51–0 the next weekend. Notre Dame's return to pigskin pre-eminence after an unsettling seventeen-year drought dovetailed nicely with my adolescent Delaware Valley needs because the Phillies were horrible, the Eagles were sliding toward oblivion, the Flyers did not yet exist, and nobody in Philadelphia cared much about the 76ers.

Unlike my father, born in 1924, whose passion for Notre Dame was fueled almost entirely by the whole Irish-Catholic, North versus South, Nixon versus Kennedy, Us versus Them vendetta approach to life, I suspect that I became a Notre Dame fan because my father adored them and because to a teenage boy they seemed like knights in shining armor. But it helped that they usually won. And on the rare occasions when they didn't win, you knew that they would win next week, because they usually had Navy. More to the point, the Fighting Irish were nothing like the Eagles, who, far from being America's Team, weren't even Pennsylvania's Team.

My affection for the Irish has survived many trying moments. I smashed up some excellent furniture in a Parisian boardinghouse in 1972 after listening to an Armed Forces Radio broadcast of Anthony Davis scoring six touchdowns against Notre Dame; I suffered through the Faust Famine, the Powlus Pestilence, and, most recently, the Davie Darkness. Throughout these tribulations, there has rarely been a fall

Saturday afternoon I have not spent watching the Fighting Irish, fully expecting them to emasculate their opponent and continue their march toward the national championship. And even though Notre Dame has won just one title in the last twenty-five years, my faith remains unshaken. They *always* look like the team that's going to win. They've got the uniforms, the leprechaun, a marching band as implacable as the IRA, the hand-painted helmets, Touchdown Jesus, the ghost of Knute Rockne. They are mythological figures in a country that's running short on mythology. And, like I said, they've usually got Navy on Saturday.

YET THROUGHOUT MY LONG CAREER AS A NOTRE DAME supporter, I had always kept my distance from their fans. I had never felt compelled to watch the Southern Cal game at McSorley's or the Michigan game at the Faith 'n' Begorra Pub. In fact, I had never felt any need to watch the games with anyone. This has worked out well for my friends, many of whom are Jews. Like a cigar aficionado who is perfectly capable of enjoying a Cohiba in the privacy of his home and does not feel compelled to puff in cigar-bar drill formations, I am perfectly capable of being Irish-American all by myself, without being part of a shamrocked coterie. Besides, I don't drink.

But as I drifted into the wasteland of middle age, I felt it was time to confront the inherent hypocrisy in my pigskin predilections. Here I was, a lifelong Notre Dame supporter who had spent most of his life going out of his way to avoid other Notre Dame fans for precisely the same reason that the school's detractors avoid them: too much blarney. All my life, I had supported a team whose antecedents stretched back to the Four Horsemen of the 1920s, while refusing to have anything to do with that team's fans. It was as if I had concocted a pure and pristine platonic Fighting Irish universe, which trumpeted the golden dome, the golden helmets, the retro uniforms, and the marching band, but which meticulously excluded the battalions of paunchy, bleary-eyed, middle-aged men with leprechauns adorning their chests, cheeks, skulls, who honestly believed that in the eyes of God they found more favor than the battalions of paunchy, bleary-eyed, middle-aged men in Razorback sweatshirts. The more I thought about it, the more I came to see that if my passion for the Fighting Irish was genuine, I could no longer shield myself from the less classy, less abstruse components of the Notre Dame experience. If my affection was tried-and-true, it was time for me to make the pilgrimage that all worthy Irish-American males must one day make. It was time to head for South Bend for the season opener.

Earlier, I mentioned the deepest, darkest pit of hell. It's the first left past South Bend, Indiana. From the obese, toothless cab driver who boasts about groping co-eds and then blithely inquires, "Are you a Jew?" to the "weather-permitting" horse-drawn carriage rides around the deceased downtown to the hideous strip of motels and bars and fast-food joints that form the general Notre Dame catchment area, this is one charm-free burg: Gary, Indiana, without all the glitz.

None of this reflects badly on Notre Dame, which sits like a tropical island in a more topographically engaging part of the city. The campus is pristine, wooded, laked, enticing. No Oxford, no Harvard, not as jaw-droppingly beautiful as they make it out to be in the movie *Rudy,* but still pretty snazzy. Especially for Indiana. A new, improved Ohio.

But there is more. For what sets Notre Dame apart from every other college football program is that it offers the visitor a complete package: iconography, mythology, choreography, theology, ethnography. Sure, Michigan has a rich football tradition, but it doesn't have any spectral Norwegian coaches whose death sent an entire nation into shock. Yes, the Nittany Lions have done pretty well for themselves, but they cannot lay claim to identification with any particular ethnic or religious group; they are constrained by their very nittaninniness. As for Southern Cal, a school whose single most famous alumnus is O. J. Simpson—brethren, what further need have we of witness?

By contrast with these rigorously prosaic institutions, Notre Dame offers a complete smorgasbord of terrestrial and extraterrestrial delights. For example, Notre Dame has a grotto. And not just any grotto but a grotto that is a replica of the one where the Blessed Virgin Mary appeared to an impressionable peasant girl in southern France in 1858. Never mind the complete absence of the abandoned wheelchairs, discarded canes, and superfluous crutches that give Lourdes its special cachet, never mind that the Blessed Virgin Mary has never appeared to anyone in the Hoosier state (the Church still has standards to uphold); when Notre Dame fans invade this Epcot Lourdes, their gaping eyes, flashing cameras, and slack jaws signal their belief that the grotto is in the same ecclesiastical league as Fátima or Gethsemane. You can't explain it; it's a Catholic thing.

Obviously, the campus is invariably crawling with the Irish, the professionally Irish, the semiprofessionally Irish, the faux Irish, the Irish manqué, and the para-Irish, just as it would be crawling with swarthy Mediterranean types had history taken a different course and Notre Dame become the spiritual home of the Fighting Portuguese. In my father's lifetime, Irish-Americans were still low enough on the socioeconomic ladder that Notre Dame's pigskin exploits resonated far beyond the gridiron. This has not been the case in my lifetime, where the triumph of the Irish-American community is reasonably complete.

Nevertheless, Irish-Americans still like to think of themselves as an embattled minority. Forty million strong, with the entire eastern seaboard in our back pocket, we still insist on pretending we're Tuaregs or something. But when one strolls around the campus and sees all those chunky Baby Boomers in leprechaun shirts, there is no doubt that the ongoing myth of the downtrodden Irish is an important component of the Notre Dame package. It's like when Cher got on that Indian kick of hers, or when Martin Sheen and Raquel Welch suddenly exhumed their long-buried Latino roots; deep down inside every immigrant group wants to be able to claim some psychic kinship with the poor and the oppressed without actually being poor and oppressed. The following afternoon, when whitebread Kansas gets annihilated, the crimes of Oliver Cromwell will be avenged and the Black and Tans will at long last have their comeuppance.

The biggest surprise for me at South Bend was the unnerving wholesomeness of the legions of fans, alumni, and would-be alumni who had made this opening-day pilgrimage. I had only been to one Notre Dame game in my life (they were playing

Navy at the Vet), and the crowd mostly consisted of the same fat drunks you see at Eagles games. But the hordes of Fighting Irish supporters who had descended on South Bend for the weekend were decidedly nonpathological. Affable retirees. Dewey-eyed middle-aged men with wide-eyed sons in tow. And lots of women. As opposed to pro football crowds—throngs of angry men united by decades of municipal dishonor and ill-considered wagers—this crowd was, well, pleasant. It made me feel out of place. Like I said, I grew up watching the Eagles.

As the day moved along, the Notre Dame experience started to gather a centrifugal force. A prayer service in the basilica. The ritual painting of the helmets. And then a central-casting pep rally. The student body screaming like, well, banshees. An African-American leprechaun in complete overdrive. Matt Doherty, the new basketball coach, vowing that the state of Kansas, which took Knute Rockne from the Irish on March 31, 1931, would feel full retribution on the morrow. Coach Bob Davies evoking the improbable dream that his young, untested squad would compete for the national championship. And the players—some smiling, but mostly solemn, solemn, solemn—rooted to their seats, anxious to get out on the field and do what Notre Dame players have been doing for a century: smashing their patsy opening-day opponent into smithereens. Finally, the band wrapped things up with the hymn that was played at Rockne's funeral. The entire gymnasium locked arms and swayed.

Well, almost the entire gymnasium. There have always been two warring strains in the Irish-American personality: one vindictive and dour, the other sentimental and weepy. It's no secret which branch of the clan I belong to. When Doherty talked about avenging Rockne's death, he went straight to the top of my list of Irish-American heroes. The mawkish lock-armed swaying, however, reminded me of one too many open-casket wakes. Yet as I studied the thousands of Fighting Irish supporters, I could not help being impressed by the epic scale of the hootiness I was witnessing. Sappiness on the itsy-bitsy rural Texas high school football level was merely embarrassing. But hokiness as all-encompassing as this gave off an almost supernatural afterglow. With the grotto, the hand-painted helmets, the Gipper, the swaying, these guys had all the psychological and neurological bases covered. I could now understand why so many people hated the Fighting Irish, who had somehow managed to transform a congenial autumnal athletic activity into a jihad. But whining about Notre Dame for being cloyingly self-righteous is about as useful as moaning about the Pacific Ocean for being too large. Sometimes you just have to sidestep the tidal wave and let nature take its course. Let's face it, what's the mileage in rooting *against* these guys?

I am fully aware that other schools with other alumni hate all this. I don't blame them for despising *Rudy,* the deceptively calculating 1993 film about a no-talent practice squad player who badgers head coach Dan Devine into letting him play a single set of downs in a game where Notre Dame already had a huge lead. (The protagonist spent sixteen years badgering Hollywood executives into making a deceptively heartwarming movie about his badgering head coach Dan Devine into letting him play a single set of downs in a game where Notre Dame already had a huge lead.) How this is any different from the Berlin Philharmonic allowing a tin-eared bathroom baritone to belt out a couple notes of Mahler's *Das Lied von der Erde* is beyond me. Rudy Ruettiger is an egotistical hammerhead, and nothing more. His movie stinks.

From the moment the pep rally ended on Friday at dusk until the moment the game began at 2:30 the following afternoon, I decided to get out of the way and go with the flow—as they used to say at USC. Chowing down at the Gipper Café, I reveled in the arguments about Ron Powlus's legacy and why Rick Mirer never achieved true greatness. (A near-great in college, but a bum in the pros, Mirer logged time with both the Eagles and the Jets. Typical.) As the weekend passed, I stopped smirking at the redundant IRISH FANS WELCOME signs in the local bars. And I completely put out of my mind what an awful announcer Joe Theismann was.

The next morning, as I roamed through the legions of tailgaters, arrayed like picnicking Knights Templars tooling up for the Saracens, I again reflected on the perverse logic of fandom. Supporting a particular team and vilifying its opponents necessitated an inexplicable bonding process whereby an army of complete strangers alchemically metamorphosed into one's sworn kinsmen. Yesterday I was looking at this outfit with the jaundiced journalist's eye, chuckling at their unreconstructed paddywhackery. Now they were my brothers and sisters. Yesterday, their obsessive Hibernophilia was getting on my nerves. Now I was ready to march into hell for a heavenly cause with them at my side. Of course, it helped that when we marched through the gates of hell together, the armies of Satan would be solid seventeen-point underdogs.

Two weeks earlier, I had experienced similar feelings at the Cathedral of Notre Dame in Paris. The two Notre Dames have much in common. Both are houses of worship. Both attract vast armies of annoying tourists. Both are famous for rituals dominated by taciturn men in highly traditional uniforms. Both are associated with cultural sight gags: Quasimodo and the leprechaun. Both have sacred beverages. Both are linked with miracles. But more important, if you happen to subscribe, at any level, to the creed associated with Notre Dame de Paris and Notre Dame de South Bend, you can feel the hair on the back of your neck stand up once they get the music cranked up. Sure, Catholics carry a lot of baggage (the Crusades, the sack of Constantinople, the Spanish Inquisition, Catholicism in general). But they definitely know how to put on a show.

Just before kickoff, I phoned one of my close friends, an Irish-American, to gloat. I told T.J. that from my scalper-special seat in the next-to-last row, I could see both the Golden Dome and Touchdown Jesus. It was, I believe, the only time that my friend, a Bronx native, had ever been jealous of anyone currently located in the state of Indiana. T.J. told me how ecstatic I would feel when the players came tearing out of that tunnel in their fiercely anachronistic, never-give-an-inch uniforms. "I wish I could be there," he said. "Enjoy it for me."

I enjoyed it all right. I enjoyed it for T.J. I enjoyed it for Jimmy Hart. I enjoyed it for my father, who never got to see the Golden Dome, for my grandfather, who never got to see the Golden Dome, for every Irish-American who never got to see the Golden Dome, and yes, I enjoyed it for Brian Boru and the Fighting Prince of Donegal. The band belted out the fight song, the leprechaun whipped the crowd into the proverbial frenzy, the Golden Dome gleamed under the brutal late-summer sun, and the ghost of Rockne stirred. Next Saturday, up in Michigan, things might be different, but this afternoon it was 1966, 1973, 1977, 1988 all over again. The team galloped out of the tunnel, and you wondered how anyone could ever think of beating them. Within eight minutes, it was 20–0, on the way to 48–13. God was in His heaven, and all was right on His earth. Just like when I was a kid, I felt pity for these hapless mortals who had been lured to South Bend, only to discover what everyone else already knew about the Fighting Irish. They never stumble. They never fall.

SINCE SCIENTIFIC THEORY HOLDS THAT FOR EVERY ACTION there must be an equal and opposite reaction, there exists another type of fan who lives and breathes green, but whose team stumbles and falls all the time. Unlike the Fighting Irish, whose bright, shining moments span an entire century, this team's mythology begins and ends on a January afternoon in January 1970. It has been said that Nature abhors a vacuum. By the looks of it, Nature also abhors the New York Jets.

On December 9, 1979, during halftime at a New York Jets–New England Patriots game at Shea Stadium, a radio-contolled model airplane went out of control and struck a twenty-year-old man in the head. Six days later, the man died. Incredibly, inexplicably, and perhaps unfairly, the victim was not a Jets fan. Still, that bizarre incident has forever reminded me of the stark perils of sitting among Jets fans, as I sometimes do. It's not just that you could get beer spilled all over you, or get spit on, or get your lights punched out, or watch the Jets lose 44–7 at the home opener. You could actually get killed.

Until quite recently, mayhem of one sort or another was the rule at Jets home games. Take the incident that occurred at the famous Halloween Game (actually October 17) in 1988. That was the nationally televised Monday night game at which the crowd went completely berserk, with some fans actually setting parts of the stands on fire. The charitable argument is that the fans were cold, but more likely they had overdosed on the kind of potent antifreeze that comes in six-packs. The near riot—in which forty-one grandstand fights were reported, fifteen fans were arrested, fifty-six fans were ejected, and five people were hospitalized—resulted in a ban on beer sales at all night games.

Thanks a lot, guys.

Even where alcohol is not involved, negative camaraderie is the rule at Jets games. Consider the fate of the unsuspecting fan I saw at a game in 1995. The man happened to be a doppelgänger for the Jets' hapless—and justly despised—head coach, Richie Kotite. Same receding hairline, same eyeglasses, same baffled expression. Yes, he did look just a touch out of place in a stadium where there are so many bare-chested, cigar-chomping, tattooed white men with long hair in doo-rags that you sometimes fear that you've wandered into an Axel Rose lookalike contest. Inevitably, in the fourth period, with the Oakland Raiders annihilating the Jets 47–10, somebody hit the Kotite lookalike with a sandwich bag—seemingly, just because he looked like Kotite.

Several people cheered. I think I was one of them. At Jets games, sociopathic behavior becomes so contagious so fast that you eventually start to feel that anyone crazy enough to come out to a Jets home game bearing a face and hairline like

Richie Kotite's deserves everything he gets. As did the idiot—me—who was stupid enough to challenge a fan's theory that black refs had it in for the Jets. If I hadn't had my nine-year-old riding shotgun, I think the guy would have taken a bite out of me. Quarterback Boomer Esiason once said that as soon as he arrived in New York, he decided that the fighting, the taunting, and the drinking were so bad that he would never again bring his family to the games. And that was in the family section. When the Jets were winning.

Oh no, please don't let me be misunderstood. I am not now, nor have I ever been, a Jets fan. But many of my friends are Jets fans, and since we do share a hatred of the Giants, I've always kept an eye on the Jets. In the past ten years I have frequently been the recipient of spare tickets to their games. And over the years, I have come to this sad conclusion: With the exception of my obviously wonderful friends—decent, civil, God-fearing men whom the Gods of Football have dealt a very bad hand—Jets fans are the angriest, orneriest professional sports fans in America. Worse than Yankees fans, who have been known to strip the clothes off people wearing Red Sox regalia. Worse than Red Sox fans, who have been known to taunt visiting black baseball players. Worse than Phillies fans, who booed the greatest third baseman in the history of the game for almost a decade, and who ran a previous great third baseman out of town just because he was black. Worse even than Patriots fans, who have been known to urinate on heart attack victims in the stands. Though the urinating seems to have to dropped off considerably after Super Bowl XXXVI.

As an outsider attending games played by a team I like but

do not love, I have become fascinated by the angst-drenched mentality of the New York Jets fan. Everyone who follows sports knows that the Jets—who have gone through eight seasons with four or fewer victories—are the most pathetic team in the history of professional football. A few years back *The New York Times,* which usually doesn't go in for this sort of thing, published a statistical analysis proving—not suggesting but *proving*—that the Jets were the least successful team in the history of football. As if any proof were needed.

Yes, it's been a long, long time since Joe Namath and Gang Green humiliated the haughty, heavily favored Colts in Super Bowl III. Still, the rehearsed masochism may be a bit overdone. Jets fans automatically think that suffering in New York is worse than suffering in Seattle, because people in Seattle don't have to deal with subways, crime, life. They conveniently forget that Seattle fans have never seen their team in the Super Bowl.

ODDLY, HAVING TRIUMPHED IN WHAT IS ARGUABLY THE most important football game ever played, and unarguably one of the two most important, the Jets' mythology seems to be built not on their one shining moment of glory but on their innumerable failures. When you're sitting in the freezing cold at a Jets game in December, the fans around you aren't talking about how different things were when Joe Namath and Matt Snell and Emerson Boozer ruled the earth. They're talking about how much the players on the field remind them of Olympian duds like Johnny Mitchell. Once, when the Jets got called for a five-yard penalty in a game against the Lions, I asked a friend what the infraction was, and he answered, "Illegal use of the Joe Walton playbook." Walton was fired in 1989. These guys really know how to nurse a grudge.

"We don't hate the Jets," another friend once confided, philosophically. "But we do hate the Jets coaches."

One December, as another forlorn season came to an end, I was sitting in the stands watching the Jets lose 12–0 to the Saints. It was cold. There was ice on the ground. We were all in a foul mood. Because only 28,000 people had showed up, there weren't nearly enough fat drunks to keep the rest of us warm. Worst of all, the Jets offense was being spearheaded by a man named Bubby. All of a sudden, a large, bearded fan in a threadbare green outfit began making his way through the stands.

"Johnny Lam Jones," he croaked.

"Blair Thomas," he moaned.

"Kenny O'Brien," he mumbled weakly.

As the man continued to drag his carcass through the stands, lachrymosely reciting this litany of No. 1 draft picks who had turned into 24-carat busts, I took time to reflect on the apocalyptic annual loss that is such a fixture of the Jets Experience. Obviously, lots of teams blow big leads and lose games they should have won. What makes the Jets so special is that they always lose these types of games at home. In October 2002, the Jets blew a 21–3 third-quarter lead over the plebian Browns. In 1995, the Jets had a 21–0 second-quarter lead against the Philadelphia Eagles, then, shortly before halftime, broke quarterback Randall Cunningham's leg. The Jets lost by four.

Ordinarily, a disaster like that would go down as the greatest collapse in a team's history. But with the Jets, it wasn't even the greatest collapse of the season. The most crushing defeat ever, the game that has become for Jets fans what The Fumble game was for Giants fans, was a November 1995 loss to the Miami Dolphins. This was the game where the 6–5 Jets, holding a 24–7 lead late in the third quarter, and in possession of the ball, decided to look downfield. *On first down.* A win and the Jets would have been in first place. Instead, Miami picked off the ball, scored, scored again, and then notched the winning touchdown on an astute franchise-defining play where crafty Dan Marino appeared to spike the ball but then threw it into the end zone over the head of the snookered rookie defensive back Aaron Glenn.

After that meltdown, the Jets' ancient, mysterious, and very possibly insane owner Leon Hess went out and hired Richie Kotite to be his new head coach. In a remark so cryptic that cultural anthropologists will still be analyzing it centuries from now, Hess said, "I want to win now." Kotite, who had just lost his last seven games with the Eagles, thereupon guided the Jets to their worst season in history, winning just three games, and the next season, one. In Kotite's defense, it doesn't seem fair that a genuinely nice man who had survived brain surgery and four years in Philadelphia should then be asked to coach the Jets.

Interestingly, the Jets are trading on a mythology so ancient that many of the fans cannot even remember when the original mythology was being shaped. What's more, a lot of the mythology is just plain wrong. Namath is remembered as the man who always won the big game. But in fact, during his twelve seasons in New York, his record was a so-so 60–63–4, with only three winning seasons. And in the eight years after Super Bowl III, his Jets posted just one winning record.

Somehow, that doesn't matter. Namath was exciting. Namath once threw for 4,000 yards. And Namath won the most important football game in the history of the sport. Well, either the first or second most important. Most important of all, Joe Namath was Joe Namath, the man who sold the franchise's soul to the devil in exchange for one brief, shining moment of glory. Most of the AFL greats have not entered the mythology of the game the way Namath did. Kids today don't know much about Lance Allworth and Jack Kemp. They have only a dim memory of Daryle "the Mad Bomber" Lamonica, whose favorite play was "Go long." All of these men are AFL legends. But, as far as history is concerned, Joe Namath *was* the AFL.

Despite the booze, the pathology, and the aura of impending disaster that infects Giants Stadium when Gang Green is in town, over the years I have developed a grudging respect for their fans. Here's why. For long periods of time, teams like the Lions, the Cardinals, and the Eagles have been horrible. But they have been horrible in towns where they are basically revered, where they are the very center of the universe, if only because the town only has one football team. What's more, the fans can suffer the slings and arrows of outrageous fortune with relative equanimity because they share their grief with millions of kindred spirits.

Imagine, then, the plight of a person who grows up in a city famous for its front-runners, yet who happens to root for the team that never runs in front. As soon as you arrive in New York from another part of the country, you realize that it is a Yankees town, a Knicks town, a Rangers town, and a Giants town. Fans will occasionally climb on the bandwagon for the Mets or the Islanders or the Devils when they happen to win, but when they do not win, the stands are empty. The Jets occupy a terrain shared only with the New Jersey Nets. But there is a crucial difference between Jets fans and Nets fans. Jets fans are numerous and highly visible in the New York area. Until last June, no one had ever actually met a New Jersey Nets fan.

Jets fans are condemned to dragging out their entire lives, creeping in their petty pace from dusk till dawn in a city where they not only are viewed as being resolutely second-rate but are actually despised. They should have been a pair of ragged claws, scuttling along the ocean floor. At least it would be warmer down there. And at least they would be scuttling in friendly environs. For to understand the tormented psyche of the Jets fan, you have to understand the stigma of playing in the home stadium of their hated rivals, the Giants. Yes, the Red Sox stink, but they play at Fenway. Yes, the Cubs stink, but they play at Wrigley. And yes, the Padres stink, but at least they stink in their own stadium. The Jets don't even have the luxury of stinking out the joint. They have to stink out somebody else's joint.

When I first started going to Jets games, I thought their fans were the nastiest, most pathetic fans on Earth, a bunch of tanked-up losers from Long Island. I still think that they're nasty and tanked up, but I no longer think that they're pathetic. Sitting out there in a steady drizzle in the dead of winter with a bunch of grown men covered with plastic bags rooting for people with names like Boomer and Bubby and Johnny Lam and Santana "I'm Not Randy" Moss makes you feel like you're out on patrol in the foothills of the Hindu Kush gunning for the mujahideen. Jets fans have a certain *esprit de corps.* Of course, it's the same esprit de corps that you find in prison, but it's better than nothing. There's a kind of desperate romance to the whole thing. Anyone can be a Cowboys fan. Anyone can be a Giants fan. But to be a Jets fan requires character. Unlike Red Sox fans and Cubs fans, who have beguiled themselves into thinking that there's something ennobling about defeat, Jets fans don't pretend that watching their team lose makes them better people. It makes them bitter people.

A friend tells a story about taking his ten-year-old son to a Jets game. The game was being played during a driving rain on a freezing cold day, and the Jets lost by twenty points to a team they were supposed to beat. As they headed toward the exits, the boy looked up, with tears in his eyes, and asked, "Dad, why are we Jets fans?"

It is perhaps the toughest question in all of sports. And yet, year after year, the fans keep coming out. To cheer. To scream. To groan. To drink. To watch some scrawny receiver fumble the season away. Or, as they did on opening day 1996, to sit in the driving rain and hail in the middle of the first electrical storm in NFL history to actually force a game to be halted, waiting for the Jets to come back out and fumble away the football—two yards from the goal line—on the very next series.

On September 25, 1994, New York Jets running back Johnny Johnson took off from his own three-yard line and galloped all the way to the Chicago Bears' seven-yard line, for the longest run from scrimmage in New York Jets history. Four plays later, the Jets turned the ball over on downs. No team in the history of the National Football League had ever failed to score at least a field goal after a run of ninety yards from scrimmage. The Jets now belonged to the ages.

As the Bears whooped it up in the end zone and the Jets players stood around in the kind of disbelief that New York Jets are good at standing around in, a fan sitting a few seats away from me leaped out of his seat, thrust his hands into the air, and bellowed, "Why, God? Why?"

But the heavens did not open, and God did not reply. Let's face it, Jets fans had been asking Him that same question since 1969. So why should He answer them now?

5

FANS WHO MISBEHAVE

PURISTS MAINTAIN THAT IF YOU GO TO A BASEBALL GAME you will almost always see something you have never seen before. Unfortunately, it usually takes place in the stands.

One torrid afternoon last summer, I motored out to Shea Stadium to see the Phillies play the Mets. With me were two native New Yorkers, both die-hard Mets fans. The Phils and the Mets do not have much of an on-field rivalry—the franchises almost never have good teams at the same time, a phenomenon sometimes referred to as *asynchronous sucking*—but as the cities generally loathe each other, there is always an emotional element to the game. And although I have not seen the Phillies win a game at Shea since 1988, when Mike

Schmidt was still in pinstripes, I enjoy going to games with my New York friends because I never have to pay for the tickets. A native of the City of Brotherly Love paying to get into Shea would be like one of the early Christians paying a scalper to get into the Coliseum.

Mets fans have an ambivalent relationship with Shea Stadium. Because it was the site of the miracles of 1969 and 1986, and because in some vague metapsychical sense it is the reincarnation of Ebbets Field and the Polo Grounds, and because Joe Namath used to chuck a lot of game-winning touchdown passes there when the Winds of November came early, older fans have a strong emotional attachment to the moldering edifice.

On the other hand, Shea is without question a hideous slime pit. All but the most benighted Mets fans (that is, some of my closest friends) bitterly complain that while second-tier municipalities like Baltimore and Pittsburgh and Milwaukee regularly get glamorous new stadiums, New Yorkers languish in a doleful, geographically inaccessible mule trough (Shea) and a vast concrete box (Yankee Stadium), poised smack-dab in the epicenter of a slum. In the end, Mets fans console themselves with the belief that gloomy, unappealing Shea is far superior to bland, antiseptic cookie-cutter stadiums like the Vet or Busch Stadium, and that it at least has natural grass. Of course, this is a bit like saying that Franco wasn't as bad as Mussolini. John Franco, that is.

Of course, some people choose to remain benignly oblivious to all this. Several Mets fans of my acquaintance are actually baffled when I bring up the subject of Shea's architectural and ambience deficiencies. Because of the ghosts of Broadway

Joe and Mookie, and perhaps because the Beatles played there, they have deluded themselves into thinking that Shea is a kind of second-tier Fenway: a dump, but a historic one. And then they wonder why their kids end up going to Towson State rather than MIT. While it is true that Fenway is a disintegrating old barn, it has a great deal of character and a marvelous location. Shea is a rat trap in the farther reaches of the city's least glamorous borough. It might as well be in Bangladesh.

Shea's most offensive feature, perhaps, is that it has retained a lugubrious, unhygienic, proletarian environment while continuing to charge fat-cat, luxury-box prices. Beers: $6. Three bottles of spring water and two tiny boxes of Cracker Jacks: $19.75. Spending an afternoon at Shea is like spending the night with an ancient, toothless, leprous hooker and then being asked to fork over $500. There was absolutely nothing wrong with the assignation. But it should have been priced competitively.

The day I spent at Shea the Phillies were sixteen games out of first place and the Mets thirteen and a half. It was only the middle of July. The game itself was rivetingly dull in the way that only midsummer baseball games can be. That afternoon, the temperature soared well into the nineties, and the sun was beating right down onto our forlorn section. At the time, I was taking medication for Lyme disease and was under strict doctor's orders to stay out of direct sunlight. I was also suffering from a severe toothache, a bad cold, and two herniated disks in my neck.

Still, things could have been worse. Since the Phillies had only spent $57 million for their horrible, bumbling, mercilessly uninteresting team, while the Mets had doled out roughly $100 million, the Phils had an excuse for being awful. On the other hand, the Mets did win the game.

Round about the fourth inning, two thuggish-looking men and two fat, charmless women insinuated themselves into four seats two rows in front of us. They were evidently from the greater Philadelphia area and were here to make a spectacle of themselves. One of the already juiced-up *femmes fat-tails* immediately began showing off, screaming, and swearing, waving her hands and rotating her capacious buttocks, berating Phils left fielder Pat Burrell for "not doing anything." At game time, Burrell was fifth in the league in RBIs and third in home runs. When did you become a Phillies fan, honey? Top of the third?

"Don't you hate it when women get drunk at ball games?" my friend Adam asked. Sure I did. But I added that I hated it even more when women got drunk at ball games and then unzipped their shorts so they could puckishly moon the woman sitting next to them. Yes, as Adam and I recoiled in abject horror, the pudgy little pepper pot yanked down her mammoth shorts to reveal her mottled, untoned, completely extraneous buttocks. Will it surprise the reader that the Pennsylvania Porker was sporting a tattoo and wearing a microscopic thong? I suspect it will not. Yes, the swamp trash hussy *par excellence,* this vulgarian chunkster had now made a bad afternoon even worse. She was drunk. She was fat. She was gross. She was mooning her friend. And she was rooting for the Phillies.

This was not what Abner Doubleday had envisioned in those halcyon days of yore.

As the woman regirded her formidable loins, I lamented how much the national pastime had deteriorated since I started following baseball in 1960. True, the Phillies finished last that year, and the manager quit the second day of the season because, as he put it, "I'm forty-nine, and I want to live to be fifty." (He also said that the best team he'd ever seen was Stan Musial.) But Cracker Jacks didn't cost four dollars a bag back then, and when you went to the ballpark you didn't have to sit and watch lard-assed pudgemeisters bare their tattooed buttocks. Say what you want about the Eisenhower era, but at least people knew how to behave in public.

The single worst thing about the unexpected lunar sighting was that it predictably left me in no position to respond. In the mythical movie *Moon over Maspeth,* ideally starring Henry Fonda, the morally upright hero would have rallied the support of the masses and escorted Fats to the exit as the inspirational strains of "The Battle Hymn of the Republic" or "The Marseillaise" welled up in the background. But in this instance, Princess Porculent was accompanied by two swarthy bisons, the type of thugs spindly old Henry Fonda never had to contend with in his films. Anyway, how does one go to the ushers or security guards and report a mooning in section 16 of the mezzanine? I know of no social etiquette for dealing with such a *contretemps.*

Moreover, every time I have tried to do something about what security guards like to refer to as "a situation," my efforts have blown up in my face. Over the course of my life, 23.2 percent of the sporting events I have attended have been ruined or seriously impaired by the proximity of cretins, knuckleheads, wangdoodles, or teenage girls. These would include the bozo sporting a massive Dallas Cowboys Christmas tree hat at an Eagles game in 1996; the thug with the cigar ashes dripping down from his ear onto his neck at a Jets game in 1995; and the lunatic who threw a brick through a subway window at me and a friend after a Phillies game in 1975. To their ranks I might also add the four refugees from Noriega's Dignity Brigades who sat behind me at a Knicks game in 1995, blowing dog whistles into my ears, and the garrulous drunk perched two rows behind me at the quarterfinals of the U.S. Open at Forest Hills in 1985.

There were also the English skinheads at Madison Square Garden at a Prince Haseen fight in December 1997, and the Mexican *rurales* who kept calling the referee an "omo-sex-you-all" during a 1983 Golden Gloves bout at the old Felt Forum. Finally, there was the Pittsburgh Pirates fan who came to Shea Stadium for a September 1980 doubleheader just so he could root against the Phils. The same day, the Pirates were playing a doubleheader in Montreal. In other words, this Iron City iconoclast would rather fly to New York to curse the Phils than fly to Montreal to support the Buckos. 858 in the SATs? Maybe 870.

My smoldering fury aside, in each of these situations I was powerless to react because the miscreants were too large, too menacing, or too numerous to risk confronting, or because I was invariably accompanied by a small child, a woman, or a retired morris dancer. Morris dancing is a colorful style of English folk dancing that involves a lot of festive clapping and jumping and the waving of colorful, ceremonial handkerchiefs. It is completely useless against four Panamanians armed with dog whistles. Thus, in all of these cases, I had no choice but to sit and suffer in silence.

I have polled many of my friends and learned not only that they have confronted similar situations throughout their lives but that in some cases their predicaments have been worse. A friend of mine was attending a soccer game in London when he happened to notice that the man standing directly behind him was pissing into his coat pocket. Relieved that it wasn't his hand, he ignored him. Another friend was confronted by a bottle-wielding scalper outside the ballpark one afternoon. Later that day, after the scalper was taken into custody, he noticed a truly spectacular fistfight taking place in the lower level. Staring through his sunglasses, he realized that he knew the assailant. It was his brother.

You can't take some people anywhere.

WILLIAM BUTLER YEATS ONCE SAID THAT ALL LIFE IS A preparation for something that is probably not going to happen. This is particularly true if you are a Montreal Expos fan. But beyond the quest for victory, the average male spends his entire life in search of the defining moment that is never going to materialize, the moment when he decides that he's fed up and isn't going to take it anymore, the one time when he's going to take a stand and face down the riffraff, no matter how intimidating, no matter how plentiful.

In my own life as a sports fan, I have mustered the courage to deal with annoying or obnoxious neighbors on just a handful of occasions. In all but one instance, my efforts have been crowned with failure and disgrace.

I have lost track of the number of times that I have ducked

out to the men's room on a contrived urinary mission, when the real reason I left my seat was to check out the opposition and determine whether they were sufficiently scrawny to tangle with. Inevitably, when I stole a glance at the offenders, they were the Bunyan Quintuplets, adorned with tattoos and Oakland Raiders jerseys, or a crew of marauding bikers, or the entire U.S. Marine Corps. Why, oh why, can't they ever be three guys who look like Pee-wee Herman, or two guys in retro lime-green polyester shirts who look like the geeks who make the staff recommendations at the local independent bookstore, or one guy who's a dead ringer for Richard Simmons? Why can't the motormouth jackass sitting directly behind you ever look like your grade school glee club teacher, now a blind, arthritically hobbled seventy-five? Where are the pussies when you really need them?

A friend once told me about an experience he had while attending a Yankees game in the early 1970s. It was April, it was hot, and the stadium was filled with suits, many of them empty. One of the business types was a drunken woman who screeched and cackled throughout the game. Repeatedly warned to shut her yap, she belligerently refused to do so. Finally, two men sitting behind her took matters in their own hands and doused her with beer. Furious, humiliated, but no less rambunctious, the woman summoned a pair of dim-witted security guards. But here, in one of those majestic moments that I personally have never witnessed in my entire life, the whole section rose as one in defense of the retaliating men and explained the circumstances that had led to their unchivalrous action. At this point the guards threw the woman out of the stadium.

Here we must come to grips with a number of perplexing ethical issues. For starters, while I enthusiastically endorse beer-dousing on male fans who have manifested a complete inability to behave in public, I do not believe that a man ever has the right to pour beer on a woman, no matter how exasperating her behavior. That's what popcorn is for. Second, the fact that it took two men to give a lone female a barley baptism suggests an even higher level of indecorous behavior. Third, it is my earnest belief that had it been a man doing all the screaming, the two men would never have mustered the courage to douse him with beer, that in doing so they were merely using her as a long-awaited surrogate for all the other men they would have liked to douse with beer throughout their lifetimes.

While perfectly understandable, this behavior is unmanly. God did not put women on the face of the earth for men to pour beer on. He put them on the face of the earth so they can ask, "What's the infield fly rule?"

I have at least one other qualm about this incident as it was reported to me. First, never having been in a situation where the public rose as one to see that justice was done, honor upheld, and ne'er-do-wells chastised, I do not believe that this incident ever transpired. My suspicion is that the beer, if it was in fact spilled, was spilled accidentally. As for the other fans clamoring to defend the two men, I suspect that everyone else in the section knew them and were merely defending one of their own against an irksome but otherwise helpless woman. In my experience, whenever incidents like this occur, the other spectators bury their heads in their programs and check the relief pitcher's ERA over the last seven games against Spanish-speaking right-handed batters at night. The general public does not know how to rise to the occasion. If it did, it wouldn't be the general public.

In any case, an event like this could not take place in the present day. With a cup of warm beer fetching a king's ransom, nobody is going to waste six bucks pouring it on a woman's head. They would be much more likely to spit. Moreover, stadiums don't tolerate this sort of thing anymore.

In Philadelphia, the management at Veterans Stadium eventually got so fed up with fan misbehavior that it set up a special court presided over by ex-marine Seamus McCaffery, better known as "the Hanging Judge." Fans who behave like pigs are escorted out of the stadium and arraigned before McCaffery at a nearby police station. But the judge, who graduated from the same high school as me (Cardinal Doughterty, at the time the largest Catholic high school in the world) in the same year (1968, the Summer of Love), says that cretinous fans now drive great distances just so they can be arrested and tried in his court, and have even asked to have their pictures taken with him, styling and voguing in their brand-new I SURVIVED THE HANGING JUDGE T-shirts. As social scientists have complained for years, this is what happens when the masses discover irony.

Ironically, it was at Veterans Stadium that I endured my most humiliating experience as a vigilante fan. On opening day in 1998, I was sitting in the upper level watching the Eagles get gang-raped by the lowly Seattle Seahawks when a man sitting directly behind me started blasting his radio. The radio was tuned to the local Eagles broadcast, and the announcers faithfully reported Bobby Hoying's assorted fumbles, interceptions, sacks, general miscues. The Eagles were incredibly horrible, and the radio was incredibly loud, so once again, as I am wont to do when I have persuaded myself that I occupy the moral high ground, I whipped around and said, "You can actually watch the game, you know."

The man, an elderly African-American, who looked like an emaciated Satchel Paige on a weekend furlough from the next world, did not immediately understand what I was saying.

I said, "The radio you're listening to is describing the game we're actually watching. You could try turning it off and watching the game."

The man was mortified.

"I'm sorry," he said, meekly turning the radio down. "I can't see that far anymore, and my hearing is bad."

"Are you proud of yourself?" asked my companion as I turned back to watch the game. "Now you're reaming out blind old deaf people. What's next? Blind newsies? Peg-legged peanut vendors?"

IF YOU ASK THE AVERAGE MALE TO DESCRIBE HIS DREAM scenario, it would be a chance to beat somebody senseless and know that he could get away with it. Think Ronald Reagan invading Grenada. When I was teenager, a coworker at a summer job needlessly endangered my life as a sort of prank. I thrashed him soundly; he never returned to work. It was the only time in my life that I ever did anything like this; it was the only time I ever found myself in such an obvious position of moral superiority that I knew I could mercilessly pummel another human being into submission without fear of retribution, disgrace, or litigation. It also helped that the guy was really, really fat.

Although I was dismayed by the primeval ferocity of my attack, I must say that I thoroughly enjoyed the experience at the time and looked forward to many similar incidents as I grew into manhood. It seemed to me that normal workplace tensions and insecurity about one's career would lead to an emotional overload that needed to be defused about once every twelve months by popping somebody in the chops. Sadly, I never again found a punching bag as serviceable as the rogue butterball. For the next thirty years, I searched aimlessly for someone who was either hopelessly fat or bewilderingly anorexic, and who would do something so personally reprehensible to me that I knew I could whale and bail on him without fear of legal reprimand or social sanction. But the blind, one-armed midget Klansman never emerged.

Then one night in the summer of 2000, during a trip to the City of Light, I stumbled upon my nemesis. Or rather he stumbled upon me. My family was visiting a friend in Montreuil, a typically ugly suburb of Paris. One evening my wife decided to go out to dinner with our host, leaving me to feed the kids. The restaurant they went to was called Le Cannibale; don't ask. Deciding to surprise my children, I cooked up a pot of spaghetti sauce, then trundled off to the local bakery to pick up some fresh bread and pastries. As I left the patisserie, with a gargantuan *gros pain* stuck under my arm and four Pantagruelian *jesuites* and *napoléons* in a pair of paper bags, I realized that I needed to make an important call to the States.

Stepping into a phone kiosk in the village square, I dialed

the number, but before I could start talking, a short, cadaverous drunk in the adjoining booth began screaming into the phone. I made my connection, but it was impossible to converse. As the man was refreshingly lilliputian and obviously hammered, I banged on the kiosk window and instructed him to pipe down. To my amazement, he pulled out a microscopic penknife and announced that he was going to cut me to ribbons.

When I went to France for the first time in 1972, my father, who had spent part of the Second World War in the French colony of New Caledonia, told me to never get in a fight with a Frenchman, as they all carried knives. What my father never told me was how small the knife was going to be. As soon as the man pulled it out, and I sized him up, I said to myself: I can take this guy. This is the asshole I've been hoping would show up for the past thirty years. I only had to deal with the knifelette.

Don't blow it, Joe.

As noted, the man was spectacularly wasted and comically short. I do not know the French word for *wan,* but he looked it. Even armed with a penknife, he was no match for me, or for anyone in my general weight class. He wouldn't have been a match for a spunky ten-year-old girl. Not with a weapon he found in a Cracker Jacques box.

I came out of the phone booth and put my one free hand on the butterfly door to his cabin. In my Sunday best French I told him to shut his mouth and stay in the booth or else very bad, very evil things would happen to him. In this instance, I was recycling Mickey Rourke material from *Buffalo '66.*

Alas, I did not yet know what these bad things were. Let's

say, just for argument's sake, that I smacked him around a little and got the penknife off him. That would leave me in a position to tap him out. But first I would have to put down the loaf of bread and the fluffy pastries. Difficult, cumbersome. Yes, logistics were a nightmare. And what if he got lucky and scratched my forearm? What would my wife say if she came back from the restaurant and found out that I had been slashed by a short French boozehound? "I leave you alone for one night to feed the kids, and you go out and get yourself stabbed!" But more than that, I was worried about what I might do to this Franco-munchkin. Even though he had instigated the conflict and pulled out the knife, he was clearly nothing more than a pathetic gin monkey. Just because he had threatened to cut me to ribbons didn't give me the right to take out thirty years of frustration on him. And I knew only too well that once we got into it, the three decades of frustration would come to the fore. This guy was going to get whaled.

In the end, my better judgment prevailed. I decided to simply walk away. I didn't have my passport on my person, and French police were sticklers for detail; they might bring me up on charges for failing to fill out the requisite forms before beating one of the local losers senseless.

I told the drunk to stay in the phone booth. He didn't. He staggered out. Half-cocked, wobbly, verbose, he began bobbing and weaving up the street behind me. I kept glancing over my shoulder, telling him to stay away. He kept coming. Looking up, I spotted a tricolored flag. Aha, the Prefecture de Police. That was convenient. I went inside. I approached two policemen at the front desk and explained that there was a ne'er-do-well or varlet down by the metro station threatening people with a knife. The cops said they would look into it. I hung around a few minutes, waiting for my adversary to disappear up the street, then went home and fed my kids.

Almost immediately, I was overcome by regret and remorse. While it would have been irresponsible to risk personal injury to myself on a night I was supposed to be feeding the children, I had let a precious opportunity to beat the crap out of a loathsome twerp slip past. I did not walk away from that incident because I was afraid of what he would do to me. I walked away because I was afraid of what I would have done to him.

This was foolish. Indeed, what I learned from *l'affaire Montreuil* is that golden opportunities to kick somebody's ass do not come along very often, and that when they do materialize you have to grab for all the gusto because you only go around once in life. Ultimately, that missed opportunity heightened my sense of the fleeting quality of human existence. Last February, on a return visit to Paris, I even took the metro out to Montreuil to see if the drunk was still hanging around. He wasn't. Once again, the French had left me in the lurch.

AND YET, THIS STORY HAS A HAPPY ENDING, FOR IN SOME strange way it prepared me for the one moment in my life as a fan—or a man—where I stood tall, drew a line in the sand, and made it clear to an obnoxious spectator that I was fed up and was not going to take it anymore.

El momento de verdad took place in Madison Square Garden

on April 22, 2001, during game 1 of the Toronto Raptors–New York Knicks first-round NBA playoff series. I had been offered a ticket to the game by my friend Adam. Adam once threatened to stop taking me to Jets games because every time I went they lost. I politely explained that threatening to cut off Jets tickets is like warning a middle-aged WASP that unless he shapes up he can forget about backstage passes to *Wu-Tang Clan: The Perp-Walk Tour.*

At the time I prided myself on the notion that Adam had selected me as a companion because I had a deep and incisive knowledge of the game and could regale him with accounts of seeing Wilt Chamberlain, Bill Russell, Rick Barry, and Elgin Baylor in their prime, all of whom had retired by the time he was a teen. Adam also owed me a favor, as I had once presented him with a framed, slightly out-of-focus photograph of Richie Kotite's last ten seconds as coach of the Jets. But in the end I think he offered me the ticket because all the Knick fans he knew realized that the home team was going to get bounced in the first round, so why waste an afternoon at the Garden? Ultimately, Adam simply cut his losses, figuring that if he gave me the useless ticket, at least I would pay for the hot dogs.

The game was an abomination in the eyes of God and man. The Knicks took their usual selection of clownish shots and played their trademark Maginot Line defense, but the Raptors were even worse, handling the ball like it was a greased Slinky. What made things particularly unpleasant was that the Knicks had given away thousands of tiny orange towels to the fans, and the six-year-old boy who was sitting next to Adam kept hitting him in the face with it. Adam and I share the normal adult primate's philosophical objection to bringing small kids to playoff games—or any games, for that matter—because they are annoying and because you feel uncomfortable using profanity in front of them. We believe that a child has no business attending a professional sporting event until he is old enough to hear the word *cocksucker* without risking permanent trauma to his psyche. In other words, age nine. I personally do not believe that a boy should actually use the word *cocksucker* until he is at least twelve, but it's perfectly acceptable to get him acclimated to the raw patois of the arena at an earlier age.

The child, to whom I shall refer as "Jared" because he looked like the spawn of SUV Satan, spent the entire first half smacking Adam in the face with the towel. Adam, who played college basketball, and who teaches karate, privately fumed but did nothing to address the situation. This from a man who once turned around and screamed at an obnoxious female Buffalo Bills fan: "Name one offensive lineman on your team! I dare you!" Yes, cross Adam Pennington, and he'll bring Lord Charles.

Frankly, I was astonished that the bellicose tyke's father made no attempt to keep the child in check, as Adam and I are large men who were clearly capable of taking the situation in hand. Especially Adam. But the man blithely refused to recognize the ominous storm clouds gathering on the horizon. Instead he engaged in that sort of paternal banter that is a staple of those infuriating MasterCard commercials: *Tickets: seventy-five dollars. Beer: ninety-five dollars. Spending an afternoon at the world's most famous arena with your outrageously annoying son: priceless.*

At halftime I went to the men's room, where massed phalanxes of the Knicks faithful were busily vomiting, but when I returned to our section, Adam had switched seats with me. Sporting a cat-that-ate-the-canary grin, his expression seemed to say, "I paid for the tickets; now you deal with the little bastard." Without hesitation, I informed Adam that he had underestimated me. Muscular men with White Sox caps cocked at rakish angles spilling beer all over my brand-new sportscoat? I would diplomatically avoid them. Tattooed Neanderthals shrieking in my ear? I would pretend they were not there. But irksome little six-year-olds sitting on the lap of their puny fathers? *Showtime, motherfucker.*

The second half started. The Knicks, miraculously, hit a couple of shots, which got the fans going with the garish orange towels, and the kid nailed me right in the kisser. Like Christ arraigned before Pontius Pilate, I turned the other cheek. *First time, my mistake. Second time, your mistake.* Then the Raptors turned the ball over a couple of times, and the hometown crowd went wild, and the Child Who Would Be Chuckie smacked me with the towel, and I tore it right out of his tiny piglet hands.

"Two's my limit, kiddo," I hissed, holding on to the towel until it looked like the child might start to cry. Then I passed it back to his father. The child was speechless. He turned to his dad with a bewildered expression that seemed to say, "Are you going to let him do that? Are you going to let that big bully rip my towel out of my hands? Don't you know that I will lose all respect for you if you don't call him a dick or smack him upside the head or at the very least call the usher and get him tossed out of the world's most famous arena, ass over tin cups?"

Pop decided that wisdom was the better part of valor. Diplomatically retrieving the towel, the ashen-faced mortal whispered something into his son's ear, something like, "Stop fucking with this son of a bitch; he forgot to take his medication."

The remainder of the game passed without incident. Cowed and humiliated, unwilling to accept the gauntlet that had been thrown down, the man made sure that he lifted his irksome progeny into the air for the rest of the afternoon every time he wanted to wave his towel. He even briefly tried to engage me in conversation. No thanks; I gave at the office.

The Knicks won the game 92–85.

Was I proud of the way I behaved that afternoon, permanently traumatizing an innocent young boy by humiliating his father in front of him? All things considered, yes. I had been waiting my entire life for a freebie like this, and when it finally came my way, I switched into *carpe diem* mode. For once in my life, I had refused to let an obnoxious spectator ruin my enjoyment. Drunks, bikers, thugs, and assorted scumbags had all gotten the best of me, and my confrontations with blind old men and mental defectives had led to abject humiliation. But when little Jared got in my face, I took the bull by the horns and hit him with the Hammer of Thor.

"Some black belt you are," I sneered at Adam as we left the stadium that afternoon. "Let a real man handle a situation like this."

The next time Adam took me to a sporting event on his dime,

it was the day Bacon Bits turned up at Shea. I think he was probably expecting me to take matters into my own hands. But having finally dealt with a first-class joker for the first time in fifty-one years, I was set for the next half century. Especially since Lady Lard was accompanied by two guys who could have easily sent me straight to the morgue. Like I say, I pick my spots. Like Dirty Harry says, a man's got to know his limitations.

6

FANS WHO ARE SHORT

NOT TOO LONG AGO, I READ A TOUCHING ARTICLE IN *USA Weekend* about a man who had just taken a young boy—his "volunteer" Little Brother—to the ballpark for the very first time. Although Señor Swell had been given a pair of tickets right behind home plate at Camden Yards (Valhalla, to the uninitiated), he worried that he might be "sending the wrong message" to his ten-year-old ward by having him watch his first game from such wonderful seats. So instead he bought a pair of tickets to the left-field bleachers—the worst seats in the house—and let the kid watch the game from there. The payoff came when the child turned to him and, instead of sneering, "Great seats, Volunteer Big Brother!" beamed, "These are the best seats in the whole place."

This story warmed the cockles of my otherwise granite heart. It reminded me of other heartwarming tales about bonding relationships between fathers and sons, uncles and nephews, men and boys, where a lifelong rapport had been forged in the flaming crucible of spectating. One of my favorites concerned a father who pulled over to the side of the road so that his son could listen to the last inning of the 1960 World Series, in which the Yankees were felled by the upstart Pittsburgh Pirates. The payoff to this story was the moment, forty years later, when the narrator, the now fully grown son, pulled over to the side of the road so that his son could hear the last inning of the World Series, in which the Yankees put the finishing touches on the feisty but doomed New York Mets. Presumably, forty years from that incident, the narrator's son would also pull over to the side of the road so that his son could listen to the last inning of the World Series, as the Yankees continued their magical sojourn into the nation's collective psyche by fish-gutting some rustic patsy.

Although I cede pride of place to no man in the quantity of warmth generated by the cockles of my heart in the windmills of my mind when I hear these stories, I will not go so far as to say that I actually believe them. To me, they seem more like urban myths, biblical apocrypha, generic balderdash manufactured by geriatric solons in the hope of inspiring their downtrodden progeny. No one really believes that Isaac was ever in any physical danger when he went on that little jaunt with Abraham. No one really believes that nonsense about Lazarus being raised from the dead—certainly not Maple Leafs fans. If we honestly believed that several generations of the same family pulled over to the side of the road so that their sons could listen to the epiphanic inning of the pancelestial contest, how come you never hear of anyone in Detroit or Kansas City making these impromptu roadside stops? Are Yankees fans the only ones who pull into the nearest parking space to grasp at the broken shards of immortality and the bright, elusive butterfly of victory? Apparently. You never heard of a movie called *Pride of the Astros.*

The other thing that concerns me about these allegedly kismetian outings is the uplifting outcome and suspiciously chivalrous behavior of the fans at the seminal events. Doesn't anyone ever take his kid to his first professional sporting event and get beer spilled all over him by some sociopath in the upper deck? The first time I took my son to a professional basketball game, the entire Cali Cartel was sitting directly behind us, making life miserable for everyone in that section by serenading us with a nonstop fanfare of high-pitched Caribbean whistles. The first time I took my daughter to see the 76ers, they lost by twenty-nine points. The first time I took her to a baseball game, Kevin Mitchell sent a sinking liner down the right-field line directly into my section. Clutching my infant to my bosom, and bracing for impact, I watched the ball nosedive and land directly in front of us, exploding the cup of warm, overpriced beer that sat at my friend's feet, drenching my pants and shoes. This was the closest I ever came to catching a fly ball.

Now, there's mythology for you.

If I have learned anything over the long, bittersweet course of my life, it is that the home team only rises to the occasion around 32.7 percent of the time when you are in attendance, slightly less if the Atlanta Hawks or Memphis Grizzlies are involved. Thus, even if you move heaven and earth to provide your son, daughter, foreign brother-in-law, aging grandfather, or "volunteer" Little Brother with a heartwarming day at the stadium, the odds of this happening are microscopic.

And yet, we never, ever learn.

ADULT AMERICAN SPORTSCASTERS, SPORTSWRITERS, PUNdits, keepers of the flame, and keen observers of the human condition are required by some hieratic code of honor to wax poetic about the first baseball game they ever attended. They rarely deviate from the script; naturally, it was with dear old dad; of course, they got to see DiMaggio or Mays or Aaron go five for five; it goes without saying that somebody hit a grand slam in the bottom of the ninth to send everyone home happy. But when I polled my friends about their formative experiences, the facts did not support the theory. Most people could not recall the first game they went to, with the obvious exception of front-runners, who always concoct some apocryphal memory—my dad got seats behind home plate from Nolan Ryan, Reggie Jackson drove in eight runs, I saw Seaver's perfect game—to justify their lifelong support of teams from out of town. Seaver never pitched a perfect game.

I do not recall the specifics of the first baseball game I ever attended, but I do remember that it was part of a Cub Scouts outing in August 1958 at Connie Mack Stadium, that my father chaperoned, and that the Phillies lost. The Chicago Cubs were 138 games out of first place that year, as they always were, and the Phillies were either 438 or 439 games behind them. The great Ernie Banks probably played that day, though I cannot say for sure; Robin Roberts may well have pitched for the Phillies, though more likely it was some stiff like Dennis Bennett or Seth Morehead. It was boiling hot; we were tethered to splintering planks in a bedouin sun field in the left-field bleachers; the whole experience lacked drama, pathos, or charm. We'd been given free tickets to a meaningless late-season game between two putrid teams that nobody actually liked, and we certainly didn't have any fun.

Perhaps, now that I look back on it, this was all part of my father's master plan. Perhaps my father—trading on his extensive connections in the Philadelphia gaming community—had actually been given tickets to seats directly behind home plate but had reluctantly decided that he would be sending me the wrong message by introducing me to such sybaritic splendor at the impressionable age of eight. Instead, at the very first sporting event I attended in my entire life, he decided that it was important that I be given a private screening of the hell that awaited me. Defeat. Despair. Crummy food. Rotten seats. Intolerable heat. A disintegrating stadium in a terrible neighborhood. But mostly, defeat. Thus, at no point did it cross my mind to say, "Dad, these are best seats in the whole place, and I am having so much fun!" He would have hit me with a two-by-four.

I doubt if my son can recall the first game of his life. But I know he can recall one fairly early on. By the time Barry Bonds—a latter-day Beelzebub—had finished setting off not one but two rhubarbs after stealing second with a 9–1 lead at the Vet in 1998, my son had consumed three Cokes, two hot dogs, a pretzel, some Cracker Jacks, and a gargantuan black-and-white cookie. Having never before witnessed the sight of seventy players, managers, bat boys, and trainers slugging it out on the pitcher's mound, he briefly lost his composure and asked if he could have some blue cotton candy. I warned him that the blue cotton candy could be his personal Götterdämmerung, but he ignored me. Later that day, back at a friend's house, I issued a second warning to avoid the rancho-flavored Dorito chips after having eaten a pepperoni pizza, cheese whizzes, and onion-and-vinegar potato chips on top of the dreaded blue cotton candy. Later that night, he said, "I really like going to baseball games with you, Dad." I asked him why this was so. He replied, "Because you're not like Mom. She wouldn't let me eat all this stuff."

"True, but when you're puking your guts out at three o'clock in the morning, I'm not going to be like Mom and come in and console you," I responded. "He who eats the blue cotton candy pukes alone."

This was my son's first true rite of passage, and he profited from it. He had seen his first brawl. He had seen the quintessential modern baseball player at the height of his arrogance and self-absorption. And he had learned, to his great sorrow, to never eat the blue cotton candy in August, no matter how good it looks from a distance.

WHEN MEN ARE ASKED TO IDENTIFY THE HAPPIEST moment in their lives, they always cite their children's births. But they only say this for the same reason that they pretend to like Joni Mitchell records or *Chocolat,* because they know it is what women expect to hear. The truth is, the happiest moment in a man's life always involves sports. Yes, I was overjoyed when my daughter was born. But it wasn't like when the Phils beat the Royals in 1980. Of course I was beside myself with joy when my son took his first breath in 1986. But do you seriously think that compares with the Sixers sweeping the Lakers in 1983? Saying that the happiest moment in your life was when your kids were born is a knee-jerk, intellectually dishonest reaction to a loaded question. It is the sort of thing people pick up from watching Billy Crystal movies. The one thing I have garnered from my experiences as a film critic is: You can never learn anything useful from looking at Billy Crystal movies. If you don't believe me, take a gander at *My Giant* or *Forget Paris.* Remember Paris. Forget Billy Crystal.

Introducing one's children to sports is one of the most delicate rituals in all of parental life, infinitely more subtle and important than introductory sex or drinking, which they already know about anyway. Who are they going to root for? How passionate should their allegiances be? Is it okay to switch teams? Should a child root for teams in all four major sports, or minimize the trauma by only following two or three teams? And when do parents know that they have succeeded, that they have imparted the essential wisdom that their children will need in order to make it through fifteen-game home losing streaks (the Mets now hold the National League record), fifty years without a playoff victory (the football Cardinals), ninety-four years without a World Series title (the Cubs), eighty-four years without a World Series title (the Red Sox), eighty-five years without a World Series championship (the White Sox), or, God forbid, fifty-two weeks without a World Series (the Yankees)?

I am fully aware that by bringing children into the world

in a town whose teams I either loathe (Mets, Knicks, Giants, Devils), envy (Yankees), ignore (Nets, Islanders), or pity (Rangers, Jets), I have not given them an obvious career path as fans. Several of my friends who are Mets, Jets, and Rangers fans—the Hat Trick of Horror—say that they honestly do not know whether they have the moral right to force their children into a lifetime of penal servitude. I disagree. In theory, a child has the right to make his or her decision and let the chips fall where they may. But the child should be aware that the chips may fall in an unsatisfactory configuration. Why? Because the child who does not share his father's passions usually ends up playing Absalom to the dutiful scion's Solomon. Honestly, kids, do you think it's an accident that my bedroom is painted Phillies red and white? You think I'm joking about all this? Try me.

When I worked at *Forbes* magazine some years back, I became friends with a colleague from Chicago named Stuart Flack. Stuart and I would spend days upon days trying to decide whether we loved the Cubs and the Phillies more than we hated the Mets. It was a riveting subject, fraught with Talmudic innuendo. In reviewing the Mets situation, we found it hard to decide what we hated most. We hated their uniforms, we hated their stadium, we hated their fans, and we even hated Mr. Met, the bobble-headed, maddeningly inoffensive mascot whom we dreamed of luring to his death, ideally in a gangland-style slaying that would point fingers away from us.

In the end, what we hated most about the Mets was what everybody else in America hated about the Mets: their cultivation of an aura best described as *preemptive hubris,* whereby a team starts strutting around like champions before they have actually won anything. (For further reading, consult the entries under "Ewing, Patrick," "Oakley, Charles," "Mason, Anthony," and "Starks, John" in *The Penguin Book of Choking.*) Say what you will about the arrogant Cowboys, the cocky Yankees, the haughty Celtics, or the imperial Canadiens, these teams had earned the right to swagger by actually winning championships. By comparison, the Mets of the late 1990s were just another dynasty that never happened.

Despite my indisposition toward the tacky denizens of ramshackle Shea Stadium, I was recently called in as a sort of "consultant" by a Manhattan woman whose seven-year-old son, Simon, had made the disastrous decision to become a Mets fan. Saddled with a father who had grown up in Baltimore, and thus despised the Yankees, and a sensible, intelligent mother who had grown up in Westchester, and thus despaired of any child who would voluntarily choose the Mets over the Yankees (*Sorry, nurse, you probably don't remember me, but I gave birth to a child in your ward seven years ago. My question to you is: Did you switch my kid at birth? Are you sure?*), Simon clearly required professional counseling.

Impressed by my résumé as a chronic loser and bereavement counselor, the mother begged me to explain to their child what a lifetime of rooting for a team like the Mets could do to the human nervous system. Willing to put her money where her mouth was, she authorized me to offer the child a plethora of financial inducements to defect from the Mets and switch to another team or take up competitive chess. She was willing to go as high as a Sony Playstation II if it would return her son to the realm of sanity. I assured her that I could probably engineer the switch for a Playstation I. Used. Damaged.

After all, I had handled this kind of situation before. And it wasn't like we were asking a kid to give up on the St. Louis Cardinals or the Oakland A's.

Once I had taken on the assignment, I began to draw up my battle plan. First, I would rattle the kid with some disturbing history. Next, I would make some troubling comments about Mike Piazza's backing down from Roger Clemens, opening the old can of manly or unmanly worms. Then I would make a few sneering remarks about that hideous stadium and the team's pathetic, unkempt, downscale Long Island fan base. Yes, I'd lay it on thick, like Satan tempting Jesus in the desert.

But then a disturbing thought occurred to me. Like Satan, I was offering Simon all the splendors the world had to offer if he would only renege on his beliefs. But Christ had mocked the Prince of Darkness, turning him down flat. Mightn't Simon do the same? I had no doubt. Since I was clearly cast in the role of Lucifer, while Simon, like Christ, was half-Jewish, half-Catholic, the unnerving liturgical subtexts here began to disorient me. There was also baseball to consider; while Simon's Baltimore-bred father would probably never forgive him for switching allegiances from the Mets to the Yankees, it had to be borne in mind that the Mets had humiliated the Orioles in the 1969 World Series, so they really weren't that much of an improvement. (If you were from anywhere but New York, choosing between the Mets and the Yankees was like choosing between the hangman's noose and the electric chair.) Yet, if he forced his son to spend his life rooting for the Mets, the father would have the weight of the child's lifetime of misery on his conscience. What parent wanted his own child's blood on his hands?

In his wonderful fable "A Medieval Romance," Mark Twain tells of a young princess who is brought up as a prince, and who is then betrothed to a young princess in a kingdom where it is written that any woman who sits in a certain chair will be put to the sword. Engrossing and amusing, the story gathers a great deal of momentum as it hurtles toward its conclusion; the reader grows increasingly eager to find out how Twain will bring all the disparate elements together. But in the end, the author sadly admits, "The remainder of this thrilling and eventful story will not be found in this or any other publication, either now or at any future time. The truth is, I have got my hero (or heroine) into such a particularly close place that I do not see how I am ever going to get him (or her) out of it again—and therefore I will wash my hands of the whole business, and leave that person to get out the best way that offers—or else stay there. I thought it was going to be easy enough to straighten out that little difficulty, but it looks different now."

Ultimately, I decided, this is how I felt about the temptation of Simon. An implacable enemy of front-runners, yet a virulent Mets hater, well disposed toward the Orioles, yet cognizant of the allures of Yankee Stadium, I found Simon's predicament entirely too complicated to deal with and told his mother to sort it out for herself. When she first approached me about bribing her kid to stab his own team in the back, I thought the assignment was going to be a cinch. Well, things sure look different now. Like Mark Twain, I'm washing my hands of the whole affair. You've got yourself in a bit of a predicament there, Simon, and my heart goes out to you. Unfortunately, my heart doesn't stretch very far. In sports, as in life, it's every man for himself. The way I see it, you're damned if you do, and damned if you don't.

Give Mr. Met my best.

WITH THIS TEDIOUS BUT ILLUMINATING DIGRESSION CONcluded, we can now return to the more general subject of sports pedagogy. On the one hand, I think it is important to introduce kids to the thrill of competition at a relatively early age. But it's even more important to teach them to develop stamina. This is particularly true of baseball. Any small child can make it through a professional basketball, hockey, or football game, because the rules are relatively simple, there is abundant action, and the electricity in the stadium provides a good deal of human theater. Baseball is another matter entirely. Regular-season baseball is a stupendously uninteresting activity, and children must learn how to pace themselves through the ordeal. Adults can always entertain themselves at a baseball game by reminiscing about Babe Ruth or Sandy Koufax or by drinking prodigious amounts of alcohol. Children have no such options. Because of this, they can only really divert themselves by trying to catch a fly ball or by eating. When I first began taking my children to baseball games, they inevitably stuffed their little mugs with food during the first two innings and then had nothing to do the rest of the game. Now, having sat through dozens of tedious 2–1 affairs, they know the drill. Hot dogs should be eaten in the early innings, pretzels around the fourth and fifth, Cracker Jacks when the woeful middle relievers are starting to loosen up, ice cream during the last three innings. Any deviation from this pattern results in chaos.

Most of the older stadiums are designed to facilitate this regimen. First-time visitors to Shea Stadium often complain about its grim, inhospitable character: insufficient bathrooms, insufficient phones, an absurdly inadequate number of hot dog vendors, interminable lines at the food stands. Little do they know that Shea Stadium, and many others like it, are deliberately designed this way. If you have to wait in line for three full innings to get your peanuts, Cracker Jacks, hot dogs, and soft drinks, it means that you only have to watch the game itself for six innings. Regular-season baseball is only meant to be watched for six full innings; the human constitution cannot tolerate any more. Savvy parents know that if they can dispatch their children to the food court three times a game and have them wait around twenty minutes to be served each time, it is possible to negotiate the arduous passage from the beginning of the event to the end with a minimum of temper tantrums, fights, shouting matches. This is the genius of major league baseball. If it did not take one full hour to get served food at a game, the national pastime would perish overnight. People who bring their own food to the game, thus avoiding the long waits, are mentally ill. This is the sort of thing that casual fans, most of them female, do. Adult males never bring their own food to the game. If they did, they would have to pack up the kid and leave by the bottom of the fifth.

I am fully aware that as a parent and transplanted fan I am a cruel taskmaster. My daughter, who wants to be a doctor, has dealt with an admittedly difficult situation by limiting her interests to hockey, culminating in an intense and ultimately tragic obsession with Eric Lindros. At one point she seriously talked about becoming an orthopedic surgeon, presumably so she could one day operate on Lindros's knees or ankles. As events have unfolded, brain surgery would have been a more plausible ambition. On Lindros's twenty-fifth birthday, February 29, 1998, she persuaded me to fly the red-eye from Los Angeles so I would get back in time to attend an afternoon Flyers-Rangers game at the Garden. The birthday boy scored the first goal; the Rangers the next five. The tickets cost a king's ransom. Maybe I'm the one who needs brain surgery.

My son, as ornery and self-destructive as his father, has opted to support all four Philadelphia teams, virtually guaranteeing a lifetime of misery. From the time he was tiny, I have halfheartedly offered him the option of rooting for teams from the city of his birth, indicating that it would be insane to turn down a chance to be a lifelong Yankees fan. But my son *is* insane.

My son's moment of spectatorial truth came relatively early in his life. In my entire stay on the planet, I have been guilty of only one transgression for which I know I will be brought to task when the Great Book of Life is opened come the Last Judgment. Needless to say, it involves Michael Jordan. One Friday afternoon in April 1998, I got a call from my friend Jill, who is an editor at *TV Guide*. She was offering a pair of Sunday afternoon tickets to the Knicks game at Madison Square Garden. As was usually the case, the seats were in the News Corporation skybox.

The skyboxes at Madison Square Garden are actually a terrible place to watch a basketball game. For one, they are located in the very rafters of the stadium, right above the last row of the cheap seats. Second, skyboxes are always filled with networking go-getters who come to sell ad space or launch a new cable station or reminisce about the old days at William and Mary when Mindy and Jason ruled the roost, such as it was. The only advantage to attending games in the skyboxes is the quality and quantity of the free food, and the fact that you don't have to rub shoulders with the animals in the cheap seats situated just a few feet below you.

Because I deeply disliked the chest-thumping, posturing, if-you-didn't-look-at-the-standings-you'd-think-we'd-actually-won-something Knicks of the Patrick Ewing era, I did not immediately leap at the chance to take the tickets. Instead I asked who was playing that Sunday. "The Bulls," Jill replied, instantly plunging me into an ethical quagmire, for it was widely rumored that this was to be Jordan's last game at the Garden.

At the time, I knew that Jill was engaged to a rabid sports fan who would never forgive her for giving away those tickets. I even made a halfhearted suggestion that she should run her suggestion by her fiancé first. Not knowing what was at stake, Jill replied that her future husband had a fistful of tickets to the Big East championships that were being played that weekend. In her mind, she believed he was going to overdose on basketball anyway and did not need to see another game. Or perhaps she had been influenced by the unforgettable scene in the film *Good Will Hunting* where Robin Williams explains to Matt Damon that he had tickets to see game 6 of the 1975 World Series—the one where Carlton Fisk shooed his game-winning home run into fair territory—but never used them because he had a date with the most wonderful (or beautiful, I forget which) woman in the world. Ladies, I've got news for you. No man on the face of the earth, and certainly not a Bosox fan, would voluntarily give up tickets to game 6 of the World Series. Few would give up their tickets to game 5. Most married women know this, but Gus Van Sant has done irreparable harm to the psyches of single females everywhere, capriciously heightening the expectations of beautiful and/or wonderful women across the fruited plain. Though, frankly, I think they should know better than to believe anything they see in a Robin Williams movie. But a lot of women never got over *Cinderella*.

Anyway, we took the tickets. Jordan, playing his last game at the Garden before retiring (he came back three years later, but he was no longer Michael Jordan), scored thirty-five points and basically destroyed the Knicks single-handedly. My son and I loved every minute of it. It was a Hallmark greeting card/Ken Burns/Eastman Kodak moment fraught with intense Mike Lupicality.

On Monday, I put in a call to Jill. The marriage was still on, which was reassuring, but as a result of her generosity and my ruthlessness, she now had to to round up some tickets so her fiancé could attend the NCAA finals in San Antonio. Shortly thereafter, my employment at *TV Guide* came to an end.

For years I felt guilty about taking those tickets. Although I could assuage my conscience with cunning rationalizations that as it was Jordan's final game, this was a father-son bonding opportunity that could not be sacrificed, I knew that what I had done was tantamount to stealing money from my dying grandmother's purse. It was base, cruel, unconscionable. I cursed myself for my shameful behavior, my cavalier disregard for the rules of common decency. Long after the season was over, it preyed on my mind. One day, when my son was much older, I, still tormented by guilt, recounted all the details of this incident to him. In the end, I asked him how he would react if he were ever placed in the same situation with his own son.

He didn't understand the question. When somebody offered you tickets to see Michael Jordan's last game, you took them—no questions asked. Dishonest? Without question. Immoral? Without doubt. Perfidiously disloyal to a close friend? Why bother asking?

"But what if Jill's engagement had broken up because of those tickets?" I asked him.

"You take the tickets, Dad. Now let me get back to my video game."

There have been many times I have been proud of the way my son has developed as a fan. I was beaming with pride the night he spent an entire doubleheader at Shea staring into the Cardinals' clubhouse and keeping the whole right-field section informed whenever Mark McGwire, sitting out a game just three home runs shy of breaking Roger Maris's record, went anywhere near the bat rack. I was overjoyed when he correctly predicted that the Patriots would win the 2002 Super Bowl. But I was never prouder of him than the day he told me to stop worrying about having once stiffed a good friend's fiancé out of tickets to see Michael Jordan's last game. He had his priorities straight; he had learned at the feet of the master; the apple fell not far from the tree. From that day onward, my son was a man.

7

FANS WHO GET AN EARFUL

ONE LOVELY FALL AFTERNOON IN THE MID-1990S I WAS walking down Broadway with a friend when we spotted a marquis bearing the title *Jane Eyre*. We had already worked our way past *Cats, Phantom, Les Miz, Miss Saigon, Jekyll and Hyde,* and God knows what else, yet here we had stumbled upon something even more alarming.

"I sometimes get the feeling that there are five genuinely awful people working in a small cellar somewhere who have unlimited government funding to dream up things that will make life even worse for everybody else," my friend remarked.

This is exactly the way I feel about the people who run sports. The only difference is: There are not a mere five people in that basement; there are thousands. The *éminences grises* who run sports work day and night to erect every imaginable barrier between the average fan and the sport he loves. In the course of a single lifetime, the average fan will be forced to hear 1,500 fiendishly unattractive young women named Maria Theresa Albrighetti take four and a half minutes to butcher "The Star Spangled Banner" before he can plunk down in his seat and see the local team get hammered by the Cowboys. He will repeatedly be forced to pay fifty-five dollars for preseason games where neither team will field a single starter and not even the fights in the stands will be up to regular-season standards because preseason tailgaters don't drink enough. Over the course of his lifetime, he will be forced to endure idiotic mascots, oily politicians, precocious *heldentenors,* cloying barbershop quartets, dozens of short, fat accountants bricking $1-million foul shots, amateur rap ensembles, fierce whores masquerading as perky cheerleaders, and the dreaded Irish Appreciation Night, where Hell's Tinkers, four vaguely Celtic financial planners from Secaucus, New Jersey, will don ethnically stereotypical tam-o'-shanters and sing wee sea shanties or mawkish anthems about driving the hated English from the Emerald Isle's dainty shores before launching into their stomach-turning rendition of "Danny Boy." And that's without even mentioning Deion Sanders, Dennis Rodman, and the Boz.

The relationship men have with sports is fraught with animosity. We hate the owners, we hate the players, we hate the announcers—especially Dierdorf and Walton—and we are not that crazy about the sportswriters. We hate the stadiums when they are old because they are dingy and ugly and inaccessible, and we hate them when they are new because they are plastic and phony and charge four dollars for a bottle of water and the retro facade is all part of a massive con job to make us forget how bad the Pirates or the Brewers or the Orioles actually are. The only thing stadiums are good for is tailgating. The only thing we like about sports is the game itself. In this sense sports is exactly like sex. Men like sex so much that they are willing to put up with women to get it. They like sports so much that they are willing to put up with Bud Selig, Barry Bonds, Terrell Owens, and any number of people named Pavel. These skinflints, blowhards, bozos, and sons of bitches have what we want. No price is too high to pay to get it.

Talk radio, itself a haven for the insane, is one of the few outlets for our rage. Here fans who invariably describe themselves as "long-suffering" can rant about player greed, owner stupidity, sportswriter incompetence. Here they can propose heretofore unconsidered trades—Randy Johnson for three scrubs—or suggest increased utilization of the Statue of Liberty play. Mostly, sports radio allows fans to obsess with microscopic delicacy about events that healthy, well-adjusted human beings do not care about. I once spent an entire afternoon at the flagship station of the Chicago White Sox listening to three passionate, richly entertaining announcers debate which was the most disappointing Sox season of the past twelve years. Not the past eighty-five years, which might seem logical, given that the team last won the World Series in 1917. Not even the last fifty years. No, the last twelve years. To the disengaged male or the average female, this is like debating which was the worst onion ring you ate in the past decade. The really horrible one at that Denny's in Tuscon? Or the one with the cockroach at the Orlando airport?

To spend one's life fixated on sports is to spend one's life fixated on idiots. Football players who rape teenagers. Basketball players who claim that they were misquoted in their own ghostwritten autobiographies. Baseball players who cannot suit up in certain cities because there is a bench warrant out for their arrest. Hockey players, period.

Sometimes, when I feel the walls closing in on me and need a respite from the madness, I resort to desperate measures. Some men turn to alcohol. Some men turn to drugs. Some men cavort with meretricious damsels of dubious ethnic provenance. Some men beat their children. I do something even more self-destructive.

I watch sports movies.

Sports movies, as everyone knows, are either stupid or dumb. Either they tell us something that is not true, or they tell us something we already know. The Georgia Peach was a prick (*Cobb*); high school football coaches are monsters (*Varsity Blues, All the Right Moves, Hoosiers, Remember the Titans*); professional football is filled with bastards (*North Dallas Forty, Everybody's All-American, On Any Given Sunday*); minorities always get shafted (*The Great White Hope, Jim Thorpe, All-American*); the New York Rangers suck (*Mystery, Alaska*). Do tell.

One thing I especially dislike about sports movies is how cavalierly they fudge the facts. In *Remember the Titans* we are expected to yank out our hankies because a team of feuding black and white high school football players set aside their differences and achieve the impossible dream. But in fact the team on which the story is based did not win the state championship that year; they finished second, just like the Buffalo Bills, the Minnesota Vikings, and any number of Atlanta

Braves teams. Wait a minute; I thought we were supposed to sneer at also-rans.

Other sports movies have similar gaping holes in their plot lines. By and large, dipsomaniacs aren't allowed to coach high school basketball teams, especially if they're as weird as Dennis Hopper is in *Hoosiers.* There are no elevated subways in South Philadelphia; for *Rocky* to be geographically accurate, Sylvester Stallone would have to be living with the Puerto Ricans in Kensington, or somewhere else in Neapolitan-free North Philadelphia. Yes, Anthony Perkins got the personality disorder material right in the supposed classic *Norman Bates Strikes Out,* but a guy who swings the bat as pathetically as he does in the film couldn't have played for the Pawtucket Poltroons, much less the Boston Red Sox. Finally, when you score a touchdown in professional football, the scoreboard doesn't immediately post seven points; you have to kick the point after, or go for the two-point conversion. Tell that to the dingdongs who made *On Any Given Sunday.*

Nothing if not thorough, I watched just about every sports movie ever made while working on this book. It was an onerous task, because I have always had a deep and abiding hatred of the genre. Here I am not merely talking about obvious malarkey like the *Rocky* films (when was the last time a short Italian guy won anything?) or out-and-out nonsense like *The Mighty Ducks, Cool Runnings, The Replacements, The Air Up There, Celtic Pride,* and *Eddy.* No, I am also talking about sports movies we're supposed to admire, critically acclaimed Turner New Classics like *Chariots of Fire, Breaking Away, Hoosiers,* and even *The Rookie* and *Remember the Titans.* In virtually all these movies, a bunch of sad-sack losers suddenly become winners because they apply themselves, because they keep their eyes on the prize, or because Al Pacino makes an extremely inspiring speech involving natural textures. In Hollywood's view, victory is not a question of talent, payroll, or even conditioning; it is a question of superior moral character and intense psychological resolve. As Denzel Washington counsels his young son in Spike Lee's aforementioned preachy but otherwise superb *He Got Game,* "It ain't the skill of the man, it's the will of the man."

But in fact it is the skill of the man that counts, which is why the Yankees have all those championship rings. Guts is great. Determination is wonderful. But pitching is better. Especially from the left side. Real-life sporting events bear no relationship to those in the movies. In the movies, good conquers evil, small outlasts big, the weak overwhelm the strong. In real life, the Cowboys and Packers and Canadiens and Lakers win one more championship they couldn't possibly need, while the Red Sox and Bills and Cubbies and Vikings get sent home empty-handed. In the movies, the long-suffering Chicago Black Hawks or gallant Toronto Maple Leafs or tenacious Boston Bruins win their first Stanley Cup in decades, and millions of fans line the streets to get a glimpse of their heroes. In real life, the New Jersey Devils win the Stanley Cup and then have to hold their championship parade in the stadium parking lot. In the movies, a tough white kid off the mean streets of Philadelphia wins the heavyweight championship of the world and everyone loves him. In real life, a tough black kid off the mean streets of Philadelphia wins the heavyweight championship of the world and then watches the city fathers erect a statue of a tough white kid off the mean streets of Silver Spring, Maryland, right outside the Spectrum. Sometimes, you can't win for losing.

Reprising our theme of a basement conspiracy to make life worse than it could possibly be on its own, I sometimes suspect that sports movies were bankrolled and released for no other purpose than to give me an aneurysm. (Or to turn my stomach. Brian Dennehy cavorting in a jock strap early in *North Dallas Forty* ranks right up there with Streisand in a tutu in *Funny Girl* as nightmarishly repellent images I have never been able to purge from my psyche.) First, they take a classic, brooding, pessimistic novel like *The Natural* (based on the shooting of Phillies first baseman Eddie Waitkus) and totally pervert its message by inserting a happy ending. Then they cast Dan Aykroyd and Daniel Stern as die-hard Celtics fans who betray their own team by rooting for the Utah Jazz, which makes you hate Beantowners even more than you already do. Then they expect you to believe that a jowly, oven-stuffed Will Smith is credible as Muhammed Ali. Not with those ears.

And yet, the more I have thought about sports movies, the more I have come to understand the important function they serve in this society. With rare exception these motion pictures portray an idealized world in which David defeats Goliath, where the massive underdog has one shining day in the sun and vanquishes his seemingly insuperable adversary. Whether it is the outclassed tomato can in *Rocky,* the principled runner in *Chariots of Fire,* the arctic pond scum in *Mystery, Alaska,* the overmatched Smurfs in *The Mighty Ducks,* the hapless townies in *Breaking Away,* the affable scabs in *The Replacements,* the doomed Parsifal in *The Natural,* the multicultural integrationists in *Remember the Titans,* the indefatigable spare part in

Rudy, the headstrong knucklehead in *Tin Cup,* the geriatric dreamer in *The Rookie,* or the feisty aboriginals in *The Air Up There,* the good guys either win outright or garner a moral victory of such transplendent radiance that the bad guys go home disgraced with their tails between their legs, recognizing how profoundly hollow their victory is.

In short, Hollywood, much maligned by persnickety fussbudgets like me, knows what it is doing. Hollywood is smart enough to realize that for every Miracle on Ice, there are fifty crushing defeats, that for every instance in which the underdog rises to the occasion the way the California Angels and New England Patriots did in 2002, and the way the Minnesota Twins did in 1987 and 1991, there are 100 countervailing instances where the franchise sinks to a seemingly unattainable new low, breaking its fans' hearts once again. In the movies, the script dictates that Shoeless Joe gets to play one last time or is at least allowed to fade away with dignity. In reality, Shoeless Joe gets no reprieve and ends his life in abject disgrace, shagging flies in the bush leagues. But who wants to see a movie called *Field of Nightmares?*

It's a story we've seen a million times before.

OF COURSE, THE VERY WORST THING THE AVERAGE FAN will be forced to endure throughout his lifetime is the nonstop blather emanating from the announcers' booth. Consider the Strange Case of Delphic Dan. At 5:56 P.M. on February 9, 1999, when ABC officially deposed Dan Dierdorf as color man on its venerable *Monday Night Football,* the sound of rejoicing could be heard all the way from the Redwood Forest to the

Gulfstream Waters. In many midwestern cities, massive rush-hour traffic jams developed as thousands of men poured into the streets to celebrate. In a number of southern burgs, mayors were compelled to declare a municipal holiday as city workers were far too tanked up to operate the heavy machinery. And in gin mills and charnel houses from Eureka, California, to Port Jervis, New York, the drinks were on the house that night.

The explanation for such ebullience was not hard to fathom. A pontificating blowhard and all-purpose front-runner who always found a way to dump on the losing team as soon as it became apparent that they were going to end up on the short end of the score, Delphic Dan Dierdorf was the one common thread uniting fans in Philadelphia, Chicago, Green Bay, and points west. Everybody who loved his hometown football team despised him. Not since Louis XVI got his head chopped off in 1793 had a long-suffering, downtrodden populace experienced such an adrenaline rush.

Alas, the fans' jubilation was short-lived. No sooner was the ink dry on Dierdorf's ABC death warrant than CBS offered him a high-paying job as Dick Enberg's partner. In doing so, the network seemed to be suggesting one of two things. Theory No. 1 posited that while Dierdorf had worn out his welcome with the highly demanding, incredibly sophisticated audience that watched football on ABC on Monday nights, his style was more than adequate for the needs of the entirely different audience of fat, illiterate drunks who watched football on a different channel on Sunday afternoons.

Theory No. 2 posited that the announcer talent pool was so thin that anybody with major network experience was worth hiring as soon as he became available. Even if he had already been fired. Ignominiously.

Well, maybe not O.J.

The United States of America is a land of truly abundant resources. It has scores of gifted writers, hundreds of skilled musicians, thousands of brilliant scientists, millions of resourceful entrepreneurs. It has 4,435 great guitarists (if you include Carlos Santana), 12,358 adroit LBO specialists, 31,253 reasonably competent deejays, and 113,768 talented lap dancers. Why then, in a country of more than 288 million people, can't we find anyone better than Dan Dierdorf to provide the color commentary during the television broadcasts of our professional football games? More to the point, in a nation of some 288 million people, why can't we find anyone better than Joe Theismann to do the color on professional football games?

In singling out the bombastic Theismann and the overbearing Dierdorf for verbal abuse, I am not impugning their merits as human beings or questioning their accomplishments as sportsmen. Dierdorf was a great, great offensive tackle who transcended the atrocious football teams he played on, and Theismann was a talented, cunning quarterback, whose wilderness years in the Canadian Football League and whose valiant galley-slave duty on the Washington Redskins bomb squad should be an inspiration to youngsters everywhere. Especially short youngsters who plan to remain that way.

This does not change the fact that every time these two lunkheads supply the color commentary on a professional football game they turn what is going to be an unpleasant experience, for half the audience, anyway, into an out-and-out nightmare. Dierdorf, more than any other announcer I have ever been exposed to, does not seem aware that the people watching games at home have on-site access to television sets and can actually watch replays in the comfort of their living rooms. As a result, they do not need him to tell them whether the disputed fumble was in fact a fumble. *They have eyes, Dan.* As for Theismann, well, Theismann is a yammer puss. And those who yammer cannot be taught not to yammer. The best you can hope for is that they might tone it down to simple blabbing.

The average man spends around 33 percent of his waking life watching televised sporting events. Logically, this means that he spends an immense portion of his life in the company of people he cannot stand. *No, not his children.* Every time a man turns on his television set to watch a sporting event, he is literally issuing a carte blanche invitation to the Fabulous Flatulence Brothers to pitch tent in the den and bore him to tears with a fusillade of hooey. Barraged from all sides by siege-gun inanities that he has no mechanism to rebuff, his life becomes an endless, one-sided conversation with the insufferable Mike Patrick, the pedestrian Tim Green, the incompetent Dick Stockton, and the criminally uninformative Steve Albert.

Then basketball season starts, and he gets treated to the bookend jackasses Bill Walton and Steve "Snapper" Jones, nattering back and forth about the genius of John Wooden and the good old days of post-up centers—this when all John Q. Public really wants to do is watch Allen Iverson go one-on-one with Stephon Marbury. Thus, life becomes a nightmare from which he cannot awake. Worse, it's a nightmare with Ahmad Rashad in it.

In the past generation, the United States has developed an amazingly diverse economy based largely on the idea of limitless choice. Responding to the public's passion for infinite variety in their purchasing decisions, the business community now offers twenty easy payment plans, forty-five kinds of chai tea, and 3,500 different versions of "Layla," which can be downloaded from a dozen different Web sites using ten formats.

Why, then, if variety is so important to us, are we not allowed to have a measure of choice among our sports announcers? Why can't the various networks empower the public by offering several different simultaneous broadcasts of sporting events, tailored to the varied needs and tastes of their viewers? By dismantling this last great monopoly, the powers-that-be could turn every sports broadcast into a thoroughly pleasant event.

This could be accomplished merely by airing three different broadcasts of each game. Intelligent people who like announcers with a bit of flair and verbal ingenuity could watch the broadcasts featuring Marv Albert, Tim McCarver, Bob Costas, Greg Gumbel, Phil Simms, Mike Breen, Ernie Johnson, Joe Buck, and John McEnroe. Salt-of-the-earth types could listen to the more traditional, no-frills announcers like Al Michaels, Dick Enberg, Jon Miller, Joe Morgan, Chris Evert, Gary Thorne, Bill Clement, and the durable Verne Lundquist. Meanwhile, the morons could listen to Dierdorf, Theismann, Walton, and Mary Carillo. Obviously, an entirely separate broadcast channel would need to be set up for John Madden.

Clearly, this is not likely to happen anytime soon. But while the rest of us are waiting for our day in the sun, here are a few measures that announcers could take to make their broadcasts a smidgen less deadly.

- Stop saying things like "In all the years we've been coming here, I have never heard this level of crowd noise in Arrowhead Stadium." In fact, it can be scientifically demonstrated that the level of crowd noise in Arrowhead Stadium has remained exactly the same since it was built in 1972, just as the level of crowd noise at the Hoosier Dome, the Meadowlands, and the Vet has remained at exactly the same level, week in and week out, for decades. The only reason it seems louder today is because you're less tanked up than you were the last time you visited Kansas City—in 1983. And please stop pretending that the fans are more excited about the game just because you and your condescending superstar camera crew have made your bicentennial visit to their culturally impoverished hamlet. The fans would be excited if the Burmese unit of Comedy Central turned up to broadcast the game.
- Please stop drooling about the Wizard of Westwood. We know you went to UCLA. Our unborn grandchildren know that you went to UCLA. But so did Kareem. And you couldn't hold his jock.
- Stop saying things like "the unjustly maligned linebacker" or "the unfairly much-maligned nose tackle." All football players who have been maligned deserve to be maligned.
- Stop telling us how much "adversity" a team has had to overcome recently. Rape, murder, fraud, the sexual harassment

of female employees, or fatal car crashes that occur because the shithead driver is going 100 miles an hour do not qualify as "adversity." It's the *victims* who have had to overcome the adversity.

- Stop talking about how a team's recent winning ways have given a shot in the arm to the vastly underrated municipality, which is now undergoing a renaissance of sorts thanks to that waterfront revival program and the steadily improving linebacker corps. The Ravens winning the Super Bowl doesn't make Baltimore any less of a dump—I went there in February 2002 just to check—and no number of Stars Stanley Cups can make Dallas appealing. What, did you think Newark had become the eastern seaboard Athens just because the Devils have won a couple Stanley Cups?
- Stop telling us that the two lethal football teams with dull coaches and unimaginative offenses are "like a pair of heavyweights just trying to feel each other out for the first few rounds." Great heavyweights actually come out throwing bombs; they want to get the fight over with. What you should be saying is: "These are two boring football teams with dull coaches and unimaginative offenses. How come we always get stuck with these sucky Giants-Cards games while Michaels and Madden get the Rams-Raiders?"
- Please do not tell us that the team trailing by four touchdowns, nine runs, five goals, or thirty-two points should not try to "get it back all at once." We've been listening to you palookas say things like that since we were five years old. The information is genetically transmitted. P.S.: We also know that there's still plenty of time on the clock. There is

always still plenty of time on the clock. This is not the first time we've watched a sporting event.

- Stop talking like a rough, tough construction worker from Da Bronx when you actually went to a twee private school in Tarrytown, New York. Let the authentic working-class stiffs like Ditka handle all the *deses* and *doses*. You getting all this, Berman?

Let me make it clear that I am not one of those effete nabobs of negativity who expects announcers to be perfect. Having grown up listening to the Phillies' banal, hopelessly incompetent Byrum Saam, and having spent a quarter century as an exile in New York City listening to the daft Phil Rizzuto, I know that there is a certain ineffable charm that is only exuded by the lame-brained local announcer. I, for one, have always enjoyed fall and winter visits to the nation's capital, if only to revel in the jubilant idiocy of the Redskins' ferocious homers Sam Huff and Sonny Jurgenson. And listening to Rizzuto try to figure out why a ballplayer's average rises 500 points if he goes 5 for 5 in April, but only goes up 4 or 5 points if he has a similar performance in September, has been one of the unmitigated joys of my life. I am similarly inspired when the Mets' industriously dense Fran Healy shocks his partner by reminding him that the University of Pennsylvania is an Ivy League school, something it is easy for the fans to forget. Presumably because there is so little ivy in the Keystone State.

But there are limits to the pleasures the average fan can derive from the predictable inanity of the men and women calling the games. Much as we may chuckle at the foibles of a

Dennis Miller or the explicit stupidity of a Jerry Glanville, there is a point at which it all wears thin. No one alive in the 1970s will soon forget the media dark ages when the megashill Howard Cosell dominated the airwaves. There is not a day that goes by that I do not thank the Good Lord for taking Cosell at a relatively early age. And, as I have indicated earlier, I'm not sure I even believe in the Good Lord.

In fairness, I'd like to conclude this tirade with a few kind words about those gallant men who battle in the announcing trenches, hemmed in by prattling nitwits, without letting it affect their work. Ever since I first heard the impish Ralph Kiner trapped in the New York Mets booth with the schmaltzy Lindsay Nelson and the somniferous Bob Murphy, I have always felt great compassion for intelligent men marooned on an island with a cabal of dunces. What did Cris Collinsworth ever do to deserve being lost in space with the rest of those numbskulls on Fox's NFL pregame show? What disastrous karma resulted in Mike Breen's getting sandwiched between the tongue-tied Snapper Jones and the imperious, belligerently unpleasant Bill Walton? And how did the thoroughly decent, entertaining, amusing Paul McGuire wind up in a booth with a motley fool like Mike Patrick and the earnest but dim Theismann? Finally, think of anyone, anywhere having to share a booth with Bob Uecker. Great seats, buddy.

In recent years, much was made of comedian Dennis Miller's short-lived addition to the *Monday Night Football* team. His canned material, his strained, ludicrous references to the Plantagenets, his ham-fisted attempts to display a genuine knowledge of the sport, his general inappropriateness and overall lack of respect for the game were all cited as reasons he should be purged from the booth. Or at the very least replaced with somebody else named Dennis who is funnier and knows a lot about sports. Leary, that is.

Yet despite all of Miller's shortcomings, he was not totally at fault in this catastrophe. In hiring him, ABC was simply admitting, "We can't find anyone better." (Until the septuagenarian Madden finally became available.) Dennis Miller, whether you liked him or not, was still more entertaining than Bob Griese, Pat Haden, Jim Nance, or John Dockery, and was in no way inferior to such celebrated *MNF* busts as Boomer Esiason, Joe Namath, Fran Tarkenton, and O.J. He was the best they could get. So they got him.

One final thought: for reasons of taste and decorum, I have refrained from saying anything about Brent Musberger in this book.

Don't get me started.

8

FANS WHO JUST ENJOY IT

ONCE UPON A TIME I WAS GIVEN FRONT-ROW TICKETS TO see Barbra Streisand at Madison Square Garden. It was a very nice gesture on the part of the person offering the tickets, but ultimately a useless one because I loathe Barbra Streisand. Actually, it is not so much a case of loathing her in the instinctive, knee-jerk way that most males despise Babs, Judy Garland, Liza, and Madonna; rather, I simply do not understand what special gift she possesses that enables her to connect with her swinish audiences. For me, watching Babs belt out "Papa, Can You Hear Me?" is like the good old days of watching Ravi Shankar trading Anglo-Hindustani sitar riffs with George Harrison. There might be something to all this, but what it was lay entirely beyond my ken.

I had similar feelings as I stood in the pouring rain at the top of the stairs leading to the grandstand at the twelfth green at Bethpage Black Golf Course in June 2002 watching the U.S. Open. The steady downpour had made the paths dangerously slippery at this massive public golf course, and all morning long emergency units had been dredging old men who had just fallen on their asses out of the mud and taking them to the local hospital. The rain was brutal and incessant; the grandstands were filled to overflowing with infuriating Japanese spectators who would tunnel under normal people's arms and legs to get a better view of the players; the paths were impassable; the attendants were useless; the food was drastically overpriced; and the Open title was already hopelessly out of reach for anyone but Tiger Woods. And this was just the second day of the tournament.

Everybody but me seemed to be having a terrific time.

I have never truly understood golf, and at this point it's a bit late in the game to start trying. I have always been aware of its existence; I have always known who is up and who is down; but it is simply not a sport I can relate to. Not explicitly stupid like NASCAR or professional wrestling, not culturally incomprehensible like bicycling, not flamboyantly Runyonesque like horse racing, it remains an enigma to me nonetheless. It is certainly fun to play; it definitely generates its own brand of drama. But because it does not involve a lot of shouting and swearing, and rarely leads to fistfights, and does not motivate its adherents to wear identical colors, it seems to defeat the very purpose of sport. If you go to a sporting event and there is almost no chance that somebody is going to burn his season's tickets or sign over his firstborn child to Lucifer before nightfall, why bother?

One thing that has always incensed me about golf is the way its fans purport to know more about their game than the neighborhood slobs who play softball or pickup basketball on the weekend. There they are at the garden party, munching on the piquant, ingeniously arrayed hors d'oeuvres, rattling on and on about their "handicap." A handicap of twenty-five means that if you play Tiger Woods and he spots you twenty-five shots, you might beat him. That's like me saying that if Michael Jordan spots me twenty-one points in a game of twenty-one, I might still get a tie out of it.

Still, it would be churlish to deny how much fun people seemed to be having out at the U.S. Open that day. Though the rain was clearly not going to stop and more and more old men were going to fall on their asses and get taken to the hospital, the fans were willing to fight for their eighteen square inches of space at the edge of the twelfth green or hole or whatever it is they call it and stand there getting soaked for an hour just so they could see Tiger Woods for three minutes. As it was explained to me by a wayfaring stranger that brutally soggy morning, holding the U.S. Open at Bethpage was fraught with proletarian symbolism because it is a public golf course and many of the people lining the fairways were locals who had recently played the very same holes. Because they knew its ins, its outs, its nuances, its treacherous spots, its unforgiving lies, they felt justified in hollering out suggestions to the golfers. "I'd use a number four" is the sort of thing they would say. "You'll never get out of there with a wedge."

Again, this is like me standing at courtside telling Kobe to go baseline because Keith Van Horn doesn't move well to his left. I have played basketball since I was thirteen years old. Not for an instant have I ever tricked myself into thinking that the game I play bears any resemblance to the game Kobe plays. I have never even deluded myself into thinking that the game I play resembles the game Manute Bol plays. It would be like a person who owns a typewriter deciding this gives him sufficient expertise to offer advice to Norman Mailer. "Use more adverbs, Norm. And stop with the leitmotivs."

And yet, it would be churlish to deny that people were having a great time out there that afternoon. Golf aficionados, like tennis buffs, seem to be fans of the sport, rather than fans of particular players, and are only looking for a good time, not for an epochal Masada or Bastogne or Waterloo—a millennial event that will define them and the players they support for the next 10,000 years. Sure, they have favorites, and they definitely want certain players to win. And there are several players—usually Europeans—that they heckle and abuse. But they don't heckle and abuse them in the way that people from Boston serenade the Yankees or people from anywhere vilify the Cowboys. They might want to see them lose. They don't necessarily want to see them assassinated.

I have great respect for golfers and appreciate that it is a difficult and demanding game. There are players like Lee Trevino who have always interested me, and when word got out that Greg Norman was having his epic meltdown at the Masters in 1996, I rushed home from a game at Yankee Stadium to watch it. I have tuned in to both the Skins Game and the Ryder Cup. But it's not a sport I am going to lose any sleep over. For me, as I have already made abundantly clear, sporting events always require some sort of cultural, tribal, or municipal connotation: Eagles–Redskins, Notre Dame–Southern Cal, Villanova–Georgetown. The contest must always entail a vivid sense of Good vanquishing Evil. And it must always entail losing sleep. I never have that feeling with golf; it helps me get to sleep. And none of the players look particularly evil. Most of them don't even look particularly athletic.

It would, of course, be churlish to deny how much fun people were having out there that day, with the obvious exception of the guys falling on their asses. I felt sorry for the players who had to follow Tiger Woods; nobody was hanging around to watch them nudge their tortuous putts toward the tiny hole. Brand names who had won championships hither and yon were out there grappling with the elements in front of just a handful of spectators; everyone else had already drifted off to see Tiger sink another fifteen birdies. I hung around for another half hour or so, but the weather obviously wasn't going to get any better, and let's face it, this just wasn't my game. I wished I could be like those teeming, huddled masses and stay out there all afternoon getting soaked through to the bone, but it simply wasn't in me. It's not that I can't relax at a golf tournament. I don't feel anything at all. Only wet and out of place. Once a prole, always a prole.

IT IS THE ABILITY OF THE GOLF FAN TO HOLD HIS PASSIONS in check that most fascinates me. To a greater or lesser extent, many of us have fantasized about being the kind of person who doesn't take sports all that seriously, the kind of well-balanced, even-tempered individual who subscribes to the dictum "It's only a game." In other words, the kind of person who doesn't descend into a psychopathic maelstrom just because his team loses a tight game. The kind of person who knows how to go with the flow. The kind of person you really wouldn't expect to find in Baltimore.

The morning after the Baltimore Ravens got knocked out of the 2001–02 NFL playoffs, I hopped on a train and headed directly south of the Mason-Dixon Line to gauge the reigning civic mood. Baltimore, never gay in the best of times, was feeling quite a bit less than chipper. A kind of metropolitan demummification had occurred twelve months earlier when the upstart Ravens had humiliated the Giants in the Super Bowl, but the victory had been tainted by the fact that the best player on the team had been linked with a back-alley murder, and that the Ravens were in fact the old Cleveland Browns, shameless carpetbaggers from northern Ohio. Still, with the Orioles intransigently horrible and the once mighty Bullets (how could you bozos trade the stylish Earl the Pearl to the lunch-pail Knicks?) long gone to D.C., the Ravens' triumph was a huge shot in the arm to a metropolis that could use all the help it could get.

When a small-market franchise loses a championship, the municipal gloom is palpable in a way it never would be in New York or Los Angeles. The day after the Yankees or Giants lose a championship game, New York wakes up and it's still New York. But Baltimore or Milwaukee or Indianapolis have to go back to being Baltimore, Milwaukee, or Indianapolis. Yesterday, a much-maligned city was the sports capital of America;

today, the muted citizens look on in horror as Cinderella's carriage turns back into a pumpkin and the horses turn back into rats. Big, nasty rats. Rats that drop a lot of passes and blow nickel coverage with the score tied and time running out.

The day after the Ravens' premature burial and subsequent descent into what is now, quite obviously, a self-destructive spiral, I hot-footed it on down to Baltimore and had breakfast at a celebrated family diner at Fell's Point. It is a wonderful, working-class establishment in Baltimore's faint approximation of Greenwich Village and seemed like a good place to take the pulse of the city. As can well be imagined, the city had no pulse; Baltimore was on life support. Edgar Allan Poe would have felt right at home.

At the table right next to me sat a fifty-something man who looked like a dyed-in-the-wool football fan, and a twenty-something man who looked like a dyed-in-the-wool dink. The older man looked dejected; he had what Red Smith used to call the thousand-yard stare, the blank look Bjorn Borg was sporting the last time he played McEnroe. But the youth was almost gleeful, bouncing off the walls.

"So, how was your weekend?" Junior inquired.

"Not so good," the older man replied.

"What happened?"

A pause. You know, *that* kind of pause. The other-than-that, how'd-you-enjoy-the-play-Mrs.-Lincoln? pause.

"Did you watch the game?" the older man asked.

"Just a little bit. I was out on my uncle's snowmobile. We were up in Pennsylvania, and he has these amazing snowmobiles he let us use."

"Well, I lost some money on the game . . ."

"It was amazing. We wrecked the first snowmobile. I don't know how it happened, but then we went back and got the other one . . ."

Thereupon ensued a protracted and detailed description of the snowmobilic arts, all recounted in a goofy, breathlessly young, urbanely professional tone I would not have expected from a denizen of this venerable industrial hulk. While the older man, increasingly exasperated, tired to steer the conversation back to the subject at hand, Kid Neige kept yammering away about his weekend in the Keystone tundra. It was despicable. It was vile. It was unconscionable. Rome had just burned to the ground, Troy had been sacked, the Hanging Gardens of Babylon had been plundered, the Sabine Women defiled, and all this chowderhead wanted to talk about was his uncle's goddamn snowmobile. It was enough to make a grown man weep. I did weep.

In our private, most guarded moments, many of us have daydreamed about taking an emotional sabbatical and experimenting with life as a screwball, an oaf, or a simpleton, if only to find out what it feels like to wear a mullet to work and still wonder why you never get promoted. Or to be Pat Robertson. In all honesty, there has always been a part of me that envies people who are oblivious to the tragic realities of sports, who do not feel like life has lost its meaning just because the home team lost. Somewhere in their formative years, they escaped from the cycle of self-destruction that typifies the adult sports enthusiast. The pattern goes like this: In the early stages of life you are simply enthralled by all the drama and pageantry of sports. Then you bond with a team. It is perhaps on the upswing. So then you fall in love with it. Then the star player puts his girlfriend through a window or gets shipped off to Phoenix or the team fails to win the Stanley Cup for fifty-four years or it decides to trade Wilt for one of the guys he scored his 100 points against, and you start to hate them. Then you get really old, and you spend all your time arguing with your friends about whether it was the 1968 team that irrevocably broke your heart or whether that didn't happen until 1987. By this time, you can't figure out whether you love your team or hate your team, or what it would take to get you to love your team again, but you spend all your time thinking about it. And then you die, wondering what all that was about.

I wish I were the kind of person who could go to a sporting event and simply enjoy it for what it is. But this only happens when I am out of town or out of the country, and when none of the teams I love or hate are involved. I once had a very pleasant time in Cleveland at a Cavaliers game where the cheerleaders did not look like dominatrixes and the fans seemed genuinely happy to have a professional basketball team, no matter how badly they played, and nobody was indicted for mayhem, much less murder. Another time my brother-in-law Tony took me to see a cricket match in Cheltenham, England, a prim spa town on the edge of the Cotswolds. This is the town where Brian Jones grew up. I had a lovely time. It was a delightful match. The local squad repeatedly hit 'em for six. The opposition was stuck on a sticky wicket. But I had no emotional involvement in the game. I didn't care who won or lost. It was a cricket match, nothing more. It didn't get my heart racing. It didn't have me calling upon the gods, the Furies, my ancestors, whomever, begging them to rain down malediction on Jimmy Johnson and

Jerry Jones. I would have felt about the same way dining at the local Indian restaurant. I enjoy Indian food. I enjoyed this. But it didn't give me migraines or make the veins pop out of my head. So what was the point?

Another time Tony and I went to see Columbia play Princeton. Ivy League football is to real football what Walden Pond is to the Amazon. We only went to the game because the NFL was out on strike. But it was a thoroughly pleasurable experience because we had nothing invested in it one way or the other. Columbia fell far behind, then caught up, then won. It was, I seem to recall, the last game ever played at Baker Field. The Lions would not win another home game for the next five years. One day I wrote a letter to the head of the university suggesting that the school pay for my brother-in-law to come over for a return visit as the team only seemed to win when he was on the sidelines. The university never replied. Ivory tower tightwads.

One winter weekend in the mid-1990s I visited Minneapolis to research a story about the newly opened Mall of America. My daughter, about ten at the time, asked if we could go to see the Timberwolves. The T-Wolves, still in their infancy, were dreadful; they were playing the Pistons, who were actually worse. Most of the standouts from the great Detroit teams of the late 1980s were gone. Yet I will remember that game as long as I live because it was the only time my daughter and I were ever going to see a Timberwolves game in Minneapolis—or anywhere—and because we had terrific fun. In fact, she still talks about it. She still talks about it because at halftime Wolfie, the team's predictably extraneous mascot, crashed into a wall while running around the upper deck and had to be taken to the hospital with a broken leg. God, it was a treat to see a mascot brought to justice.

Then, early in the fourth quarter, the farmers who were sitting behind us started asking each other why the T-Wolves never ran the old "picket fence." Well, fellers, because basketball is no longer played with a peach basket. The home team won the game by two points; Dennis Rodman had his typical stat line: two points, twenty-four rebounds; much highlight film ineptitude was witnessed. It was a delightful evening, unlike anything I had ever seen in Philadelphia or New York or Boston, where the solemn, joyless fans wear their pathologies on their sleeves. It was fun. Pure fun. Wasn't that enough?

No.

It wasn't enough because one team lost, and in my estimation defeat is *always* a sign of moral weakness, even if the other team has a $130-million payroll and is a million times better than the team you support. So you couldn't just write it off as entertainment. Vince Lombardi once told his players, "What each and every one of you must understand is that, as talented individuals, you have an absolute moral responsibility to perfect those talents with which you have been gifted and entrusted." Unfortunately, he did not give this speech to the Eagles. If he had, they would recognize that in sports the future of mankind is always hanging in the balance when a team takes the field. Well, maybe not if the Bengals are in town.

ONCE, DURING A TRIP TO EDINBURGH, I WAS LUCKY enough to get tickets to see one of the Six Nations rugby matches between Scotland and France. In Scotland, as in

England, violence is the norm at soccer games; a person wearing Celtic (Catholic) green is taking his life into his own hands if he, wanders into the Glasgow neighborhood where the Protestant Rangers play. But rugby is another matter entirely. In the parlance of the locals, soccer is a sport played by gentlemen for thugs, whereas rugby is a sport played by thugs for gentlemen. Actually, I think both sports are played by thugs for a mixture of thugs and gentlemen. Whatever the truth of the matter, the mood in Edinburgh was positively jubilant the day of the game. Because Edinburgh is a relatively small city (population 500,000), when 67,000 fans descend on the town for one of these matches it seems like everyone in Scotland is going to the stadium.

Hordes of middle-aged Frenchmen dressed in red-white-and-blue capes with massive red berets wandered through the highways and byways of the city, where the Scots, far from abusing them, went out of their way to be friendly. The Scots and the French are ancient allies, of course, temperamentally united by their hatred of the English. (Before Scotland-England matches, the pubs of the city are filled to overflowing with young men watching *Braveheart*. As the English are usually very good and the Scottish team very bad, the Scots generally don't get off much better now than they did in 1305, when the English hanged, drew, and quartered William Wallace—after first castrating him, a juicy bit that got left out of the movie.)

In the streets of Edinburgh, from nine in the morning until three in the afternoon, bagpipes could be heard everywhere. A mood of festive inebriation permeated the city, the French and the Scots mixing quite amiably. After lunch, the masses of now drunken spectators lurched toward the stadium, each nation singing its national song. Many of the French were decked out like the Three Musketeers; literally scores of the Scots had their faces painted blue and were wearing one-size-fits-all tam-o'-shanters with fake red hair streaming from the back. The entire city was bedecked in kilts. The atmosphere was a dainty pastiche of ebullience, inebriation, borderline transvestism, and affable dementia. When the introductions were made and the bagpipers slipped into high gear, the mood turned even more raucous. There were marching bands, dancers, ludicrous getups as far as the eye could see. Oh, it was quite the pageant, all right.

The game began, and the Scots got hammered. The French could have scored at will all afternoon but seemed content not to lay it on too thick. In the stands the French sang the "Marseillaise" after each tally, while the Scots tried to fight back with their own wan national anthem. My hosts—three rugby-crazed Scottish boys—conceded that the Scottish national anthem was not an especially inspiring tune, that the French had them beat hands-down in that department. More to the point, the Scots didn't score often enough to make it worth singing.

Given the remarkable quantities of alcohol that were being consumed, you would have thought that the mood here would be like Monday night at a Redskins-Cowboys game. It was not. The French and the Scots sat cheek by jowl in the stands, waving their banners, belting out their songs, and no one tried to garotte anyone. Whereas a Redskins-Cowboys game would be punctuated by fights, recriminations, racial epithets, and shouts of "Dallas sucks," the types of exclamations I heard in Edinburgh were:

"Go Scotland!"

"Take it away, Scotland!"

"Come on, Scotland!"

"You can do better, Scotland!"

You can do better, Scotland? What happened to "Friggin' French Frogs"?

Blimey.

After the Scots had been polished off, everyone rose as one and applauded the players. The French, whose squad would upset the English and win the coveted championship of the Six Nations later that month, were justifiably overjoyed. But the Scots, though disappointed, did not start a riot. They seemed resigned to the fact that the better team had won. They filed out of the stadium, made the long trek back to central Edinburgh, and got even more plastered. Many Frenchmen joined them. There were lusty toasts to be made, many interesting chats to be had, innumerable tall tales to be told. And, like I said, it helped that they all really hate the English.

In my fifty-one years on the planet, I had seen nothing like this. I had seen crowds that were listless, crowds that were disconsolate, crowds that were bored. But I had never seen this many intoxicated people accept defeat with such aplomb. The throng had spent a perfectly pleasant afternoon watching twenty-two world-class rugby players beat the crap out of one another, and the fact that the home team lost the game did not make them feel vindictive or suicidal. Why, oh why, I asked myself, couldn't sports always be like this?

After the game, I clambered into a phone booth to call my

friend Rob in New Jersey. I told him about the citywide zaniness, the garish costumes, the painted faces, the *Braveheart* getups, the Frenchmen in their ridiculous cat-in-the-hat *chapeaux*. I told him that it was one of the most amazing events I had seen in my entire life, a sporting contest where the best team won and the result didn't send anyone back to his house to beat his wife or put a gun to his head. I told him that I had seen no fights, no stranglings, no thugs wandering around with chains or broken bottles, and that after the game, the 67,000 fans rose as one and applauded the humbled Scottish team.

There was silence at the other end of the line.

Then Rob, who has been rooting for the Eagles since 1958, spoke. His words were succinct and well-chosen: "Joe, I've got just one question. What is wrong with those people?"

TWO WEEKS LATER, I ATTENDED AN ARSENAL–TOTTENHAM Hotspurs game at Highbury Park in London. As previously noted, my father-in-law and brother-in-law were Arsenal fans, so I inherited this allegiance when I met my wife. It is relatively easy for an American to pick up the protocol at a foreign sporting event; simply ask your neighbor who you are supposed to hate and how much you are supposed to hate them, and you're all set. If you support Arsenal, you are expected to loathe Manchester United—the New York Yankees of soccer—as well as Liverpool and Everton; teams like Newcastle and Queen's Park Rangers you can merely despise; hopeless squads like Derby County and Leicester you can just flat out ignore.

Arsenal and Tottenham play only a few miles apart from

each other, so naturally their fans hate each other more than the Armenians hate the Turks. Before the game, the entire delegation of 3,000 Spurs fans must be escorted into the stadium by a phalanx of ornery, stressed-out police; a seamless strip of coppers' green plastic vests separates them from the Arsenal fans. Though English soccer fans are commonly depicted as violent hooligans, Arsenal has a rather middle-class constituency. The woman who accompanied me to the game works at the Institute for Contemporary Art, where two Dutch anorexics had just completed a controversial performance-art piece in which they offered one another peanuts as snacks. Her husband was a graphic designer. The crowd was full of ordinary-looking Brits, lots of women, tons of harmless-looking kids. But from the opening kickoff, the Arsenal supporters serenaded the opposition and its fans with a continuous stream of abuse. They called them wankers. They called them fucks. They called them evil scum.

This went on for two solid hours. And even though the Spurs had a crummy team and had no business keeping the match competitive, when the Gunners finally beat them on a penalty shot right in front of my section, the general feeling in the stadium was not relief, but a palpable sensation that evil had been defeated, Moloch slain, Goliath's hideous head planted on the closest available pike. People were screaming. People were swearing. People were making weird guttural noises. The disconsolate visiting fans had to be escorted out of the stadium by even more police. Imagine if they had won.

What an amazing contrast with the experience in Scotland two weeks earlier! How childishly these fans were behaving. How cruel and unkind were the epithets that rained down on the opposition's head. How very, very seriously they were taking what was, after all, only a game. The impression they conveyed was that if Arsenal had lost the match, the sun would not come up in the morning. Or ever. The raging sea of Gunner supporters was delirious, crazed, immersed in a froth of psychopathic lunacy.

It was great to be back.

9

FANS WHO WALK AWAY

I WAS MINDING MY OWN BUSINESS IN WASHINGTON, D.C., one summer evening when a man suddenly reared up in front of me. He was my general age, my general size, with curly black hair and a radiant smile that I had not seen in thirty years.

"Remember me?" he asked.

Of course I did. When my family moved out of the East Falls housing project in 1963 and into a three-bedroom house in the more prosperous community of West Oak Lane, Richie Giardinelli was the first person to befriend me. Our houses were fifty yards apart, directly across from St. Benedict's Church, the first modern Catholic church I had ever seen. St. Benedict's had once been a reasonably upscale parish; it actually had a monsignor as a rector, a crusty old varmint from Ireland. Monsignor Collis had made the always difficult task of assimilating oneself into a new neighborhood that much harder by visiting the seventh and eight grades a week before we arrived and telling everyone that as the Queenans were the first white people to move into the neighborhood in the last three years, everyone should be extra nice to us.

This did not go down well with the white kids—what made us so special?—but it went down even less well with the swelling numbers of black kids in the school. It was not going to be easy making hard friends. Richie was the exception. I met him around twilight out on Twentieth Street, a sliver that connected the more well-traveled Stenton and Chelten Avenues. The gap between the two busy streets was about the size of a pee-wee football field; the crosswalks, I would soon discover, made truly excellent end zones. Over the next few years, Richie and Mike Craig and Frank Gallagher and Joe Altieri and Stevie White and I would repeatedly try to impale defenders on the fins of the monstrous Buicks and Pontiacs parked along the curbs. We were too young to know that these death-defying afternoon games—try to run the man guarding you directly into the path of the K bus—were as close to Paradise as we would ever get. But I think we had suspicions.

The night we met, Richie was all by himself, playing step ball. This was a popular Philadelphia game that involved bouncing a ball high off the steps that led to the alleyway. Anything that was not caught was a single, except for balls that reached the curb on the far side of the street. Those were home runs. There may have been doubles and triples, as well; I do not recall. What I do recall is that Richie immediately introduced himself and invited me to play. I had just left a poor neighborhood where I had a job and friends and a girlfriend. I had moved to a slightly better neighborhood where I knew absolutely no one. Richie threw me a life preserver.

Nineteen sixty-three was the year the Phillies traded the popular Don Demeter for the aging Jim Bunning, who the next year would lead the Phillies to within an eyelash of the World Series. Until John F. Kennedy died in November, 1963 was the happiest year in my life, because the Phillies, picked to finish last, unexpectedly finished fourth. The year a team performs well completely out of the blue is always the most enjoyable time for the fan; it is the next season, when the expectations are high, that the nail biting, novenas, and heavy drinking start. When teams are on their way up, you can blithely write off their failures as the mistakes of youth. When teams are picked to compete for the title, their failures assume biblical proportions.

When people think of Philadelphia Italians, they always conjure up shopworn images of a surly Sylvester Stallone careening around dimly lit South Philadelphia streets sporting a stupid hat and snarling, "Yo, Adrian." But none of the Italians I grew up with were like that. Meeting Richie and his family gave me a free pass out of the guilt-drenched Amero-Celtic Nightmare I'd been born into and into a miraculous new world where people laughed and sang and cooked food all day and felt passionately about everything. It was a world where fathers adored, not merely tolerated, their male offspring. It was a world with mysterious words like *prosciutto* and *ma'don,* a world where people did not buy their meats at the local A&P but at cavernous, strange-smelling establishments named

Silenzi's. It was a world where canned foods did not exist, where cabbage was not automatically consumed with every meal, where people actually seemed to enjoy being alive. For me, it was an exotic oasis in a brutally prosaic childhood. It may be true that the Irish saved civilization. But the Italians saved me.

There were only two things about Richie that I did not approve of. Well, three, if you count his affection for Frankie Valli and the Four Seasons. The night I met him he was wearing a blue Dodgers cap. The Dodgers had just won the World Series, beating the Yankees in seven games behind Sandy Koufax, Don Drysdale, Maury Wills, and the Davis brothers. People in Philadelphia didn't root for the Dodgers back in those days; the Age of the Front-runner was still years in the future. Moreover, the year I moved to West Oak Lane was the year the Phillies had their nearly magical season. Richie, depressed that the Dodgers finished fourth, did not get to participate in the general euphoria of that season. But he also escaped the trauma of the ten-game losing streak, and the infamous collapse. This did not seem fair.

The other thing I didn't like was Richie's affection for the Villanova Wildcats. From the time I met him I knew I was eventually going to St. Joseph's College, because everybody on my side of the family went to St. Joseph's, and students at St. Joseph's College hated Villanova. St. Joseph's, poised at the edge of West Philadelphia, had always prided itself on being a blue-collar establishment. Villanova, located on the patrician Main Line, was a prissy, suburban institution that thought it was better than the other colleges in the area. Richie, who went to Vietnam after high school, never had any intention of going to Villanova, but he enthusiastically supported the school anyway. In my eyes, this was some strange, inexplicable form of treason. On the other hand, neither of us rooted for La Salle College, which was right down the street and provided one of my father's many short-lived jobs. So what the hell was I rattling on about?

In the winter of 1970, Richie headed off to Vietnam, and my family moved out of the neighborhood. Richie and I saw each other once or twice in the next few years, but then we drifted apart. I went to college, then to France, then moved to New York. Richie moved into the broadcasting field, finally hitting the big time as an editor at CBS News. For thirty years, we did not lay eyes on one another. Then, that humid evening in Washington, our paths crossed again. Phone numbers were exchanged; vague plans for a meeting were sketched out.

Sometime after that I came to Washington on business. I arrived a day early so I could spend the day with my childhood friend. He picked me up at Union Station in his massive, stylish Cadillac, and we drove to his home in North Bethesda, Maryland. On the way out, he filled me in on the events of the past three decades. He told me about his twin brothers, married with college-age children, and about his parents, diehards who still lived in the same house in the same neighborhood. There certainly weren't many Italians left on Chelten Avenue, but they weren't leaving. It was their home; they were there for the duration.

As we walked into his apartment, my eyes immediately spied a framed *Sports Illustrated* cover depicting Villanova's epic triumph over the previously invincible Georgetown Hoyas on April 1, 1985. I had the same photograph in my office, but it was tucked away in a sports treasure chest, not displayed on the walls. I had been happy that Villanova won, because they were technically a Philadelphia team, but not so carried away that I would actually put their photo on the wall. I felt the way the English, Australians, Canadians, and Americans must have felt about the French after the war; yes, in the narrow sense of the term they were our "allies." But no way in hell was anyone putting a framed photograph of Charles de Gaulle over the mantlepiece.

On the living room wall was a large poster of the Boys of Summer, the 1955 Dodgers team that finally beat the Yankees and then broke Brooklyn's heart by moving to Los Angeles two years later. From the looks of things, Richie's allegiances hadn't shifted very much over the years.

But oh, how appearances can deceive. When I asked my old friend what he thought of the current Dodgers manifestation, he told me that he no longer followed baseball.

I looked across at his wife, speechless.

"I was as surprised as you are," she said. "I never thought I'd live to see it happen. Not Richie."

But it happened. In the early nineties, during one of baseball's numerous work stoppages, Richie was covering a press conference at Union Station, Washington. At the time, technicians like him were without a contract. In other words, guys getting ready to go out on strike were covering a strike. As he recalled it, Senator John McCain approached the podium and said that he and his colleagues were going to burn the midnight oil to see that the players got back to work. The entire U.S. Senate was going to roll up their sleeves and get their fellow millionaires back on the playing fields; the people working the cameras could fend for themselves. That was it for Richie.

From that point onward, he had no further interest in the sport. He folded his tent.

Obviously, I found this hard to believe. I pumped his wife for more information. She told me that from the moment Richie announced his new philosophy she was as stunned as I was. She said that her husband would occasionally watch tapes of old games on the classic sports network but paid no attention to contemporary events. He was a man of principle.

For years I had been trying to locate a single person who had successfully walked away from sports. According to Eliot Asinof, author of *Eight Men Out,* Ring Lardner was so devastated by the Black Sox scandal that he stopped writing about baseball and actually gave up going to baseball games. Given the subsequent history of the White Sox, he had probably made a wise choice. But that was a decision reached by a bitter, middle-aged man after a team he loved deliberately chose to throw the World Series. Richie's situation was different.

One friend told me that his college roommate, an athlete himself, had been so crushed by John Starks's 2 for 17 performance in game 7 of the 1994 NBA finals that he stopped following sports for good. But the man still coached his son's soccer team, meaning that some lingering affection for the thrill of competition had survived. Another old friend briefly stopped watching Eagles games because he was disgusted by the boorish, self-congratulatory antics of Buddy Ryan's underachieving teams, but once Ryan was fired, he returned to the fold.

My brother-in-law Tony, who used to attend the Rugby League finals at Twickenham every year, was so furious when his beloved Gloucester Cherry & Whites turned professional that he stopped attending their games for good. Instead, he switched his allegiances to Barnstable, a poky amateur club located 130 miles from his home. Every other Saturday, Tony motors down to Devon and spends the afternoon attending games played by old men who were never very good and young men who are not much better. To me, this is like turning down tickets to watch the Yankees play the Red Sox and going to see the Wilmington Blue Hens square off against the Harrisburg Senators. But Tony is a man of principle. One hundred and thirty miles is an enormous distance in Britain, where much of the trip is along narrow local roads. But this is how Tony feels about the matter. He has walked away from the team he followed since he was a child, and knowing him as I do, he will not be walking back.

Still, he has not given up sports per se. He continues to follow the national rugby teams, cricket, and, to a very minor extent, soccer.

What made Richie's bold gesture so dramatic was that he had literally turned his back on sports completely. This resonated with me. Many, many times I had thought about walking away from sports. For brief periods of time, I actually had walked away or had at least taken a brief sabbatical. In 1973, my friend Rob and I got so bored and fed up with the stultifying hegemony exercised over professional football by the Miami Dolphins that we skipped the Super Bowl and spent the entire afternoon riding around in his car. This was unspeakably stupid. Nineteen seventy-three was the year that kicker Garo Yepremian foolishly grabbed a blocked kick and tried to pass it, only to have it intercepted by Mike Bass and run back for a Redskins touchdown. It was a thoroughly appalling Super

Bowl—I have seen tapes of it—but I have never forgiven myself for missing that play as it was happening. I have never missed another Super Bowl. I don't think I have ever missed another down of a Super Bowl game.

A New York sportswriter once admitted that he had turned off his television the night the Mets pulled off their miraculous comeback against the Red Sox in October 1986, but insists that watching it on tape was just as much fun. No, it wasn't. It would be like watching the Second Coming on tape delay. In 1986 you had to be there to see it happening while it was happening. And even while it was happening, you couldn't believe it was happening. No true Mets fan, and indeed, no true baseball fan, could ever forgive himself for jumping ship that night; in the recesses of their hearts they know that God will not overlook their perfidy that October evening. I personally know three Mets fans who betrayed Mookie Wilson thrice before the cock crowed twice that evening; if God has misplaced their names, I will be more than happy to provide them, come Last Judgment time.

IS ALL THIS VINDICTIVENESS AND COMPULSION HEALTHY? Is it an effective use of an adult male's time? Couldn't those days/weeks/decades be better spent doing something else? And what do people who do not follow sports do with all those extra hours? Most of my friends who have little or no interest in sports say that they did not play them as children and have no interest in following sports from afar. Sports was heroin; they'd simply never gotten hooked. Others maintain that because they grew up in the 1960s, where a contempt for jocks was *de rigeur* in left-wing circles, they have always associated sports with Mom, apple pie, and Nixon. Nixon is long gone, but the stigma remains.

Among nonfans, there seems to be a general feeling that following sports is a colossal waste of time. They can't understand the concept of calling a friend from the other side of the country and having him hold the phone against the radio to hear the last half inning of a game. Well, the pennant was on the line. They can't understand why a person would bribe a friend to drive him seventy miles all the way across the French countryside to get the latest *Herald Tribune*. Well, the Phils were playing an important doubleheader. They can't understand why anyone would refuse to speak to his sister for months on end because she had blurted out the results of the Wimbledon final he was planning to watch on tape delay. (Screw you, Borg.) And they certainly can't understand why a grown man would refuse to let his wife buy a lovely house in a quaint Philadelphia suburb because an adjacent hill blocked clear reception of New Orleans Saints games. (That wasn't me, but a guy I met in my travels. Frankly, that one has even me a bit worried.) To them, such obsessive behavior is unhealthy, infantile, antisocial, and, more to the point, pointless.

This may be true. But I suspect that in refusing to waste their time following sports, these individuals have simply found other ways to fritter away their time. One man I know reads a lot of science fiction. This is a complete waste of time. Another devotes every free minute to kayaking on the Hudson. An even bigger waste of time, and more dangerous. Still others spend Saturday and Sunday afternoons watching independent movies like *Trees Lounge* and *Clerks.* Compared to this, taking in a rain-delayed Devil Rays–Royals game is a positively Heisenbergian intellectual activity. All of the above confirms my long-held belief that life is like a jigsaw puzzle we are given at birth; by the time we die each of us has figured out a way to assemble all the pieces in some random figuration, but it never, ever looks like the painting on the front of the box.

THE NIGHT THE FLYERS COMPLETED THEIR SHAMEFUL COLlapse against the New Jersey Devils in the 2000 NHL semifinals, blowing a seemingly insurmountable 3–1 lead, with two of the last three games played in Philadelphia, I went through my closets and gathered all my Philadelphia Flyers sports regalia. Determined to make a clean sweep of it, I also stuck into a plastic bag my Charles Barkley rookie shirt, my Scott Rolen jersey, and an Eagles winter jacket I had purchased for half price at a sporting goods shop across the street from Wrigley Field. The next day, I dropped off the whole kit and caboodle at the Salvation Army. *Finito. Kaput. Sayonara. No mas.*

Subconsciously, I had been contemplating this move for many years. I had come close in 1978, when Garry Maddux dropped that fly ball in center field against the Dodgers, handing the Dodgers the pennant. I had come close in the early 1980s, when the Phillies, Flyers, 76ers, and Eagles all blew championships they should have won. I had come close in 1993, when Mitch Williams served up that Series-winning homer to Joe Carter. And I had come close in 1997, when the Flyers went into the tank and got swept out of the Stanley Cup finals by the Red Wings. But this time, I was making a clean break. I was through with my teams. I was through with sports. No more heartbreak. No more kicks in the teeth. It was over; I was out.

I am not a man of principle. Or let's just say that my principles are astonishingly flexible. And so, just three days later, when the Indiana Pacers beat the Knicks and went to the NBA finals, I was hooked again. Valiant but outclassed, Reggie Miller and his feisty entourage put up a respectable fight against the far more talented Lakers. As so often happens in sports, I had discreetly pinned my dreams to a proxy squad as soon as my own team got bounced from the playoffs, in this case salving the bitter wounds of the Flyers debacle with the prospect of a Pacers upset. Needless to say, the Pacers lost the series, but by the time they did I was already regretting my decision to get rid of all that sports regalia. My apparently sincere attempt to walk away from sports and find something better to do with my time had been a crashing failure. There *is* nothing better to do with your time. I'm sorry; it is a sad admission for a man who has actually read *Ulysses* to make, but it is true. I tried to cut all ties. I tried to walk away. But Reggie Miller hit a couple of timely jumpers, and the nightmare recommenced. I was out, but they dragged me back in.

In the years since I embarked on my brief, pathetic attempt to get sports out of my system, I have come to understand why I will never be able to say good-bye. There are two reasons. One is the Bye Week. The other is the Silence.

In Philip Roth's brilliant *The Great American Novel*, there is a scene where a woman tries to get a ballplayer to tell her that he loves her more than anything else in the whole world. The man says he still prefers a triple. Money is great. Fame is wonderful. The love of a good woman is priceless. But nothing on the face of the earth is better than a triple. As he phrases it, "I can't tell a lie, Angela. There just ain't nothin' like it."

I feel the same way about the Bye Week. When your football team wins on Sunday afternoon, the sun never shines brighter than it does the next day. In other sports, the afterglow of victory can be dissipated the following afternoon; in baseball, by the second half of the doubleheader. But in football, it lasts seven days—six if you play on Monday night, ten if you play on Thursday. Better still, if your team wins on Sunday and has a bye the following week, it means that you have fourteen full days to bestride the universe like a colossus, a full two weeks to not be neurotic. I have asked my friends who do not like sports what corresponding pleasure they have ever known in life. They do not understand the question.

Well, they should. The only elation a man can experience that can possibly surpass the joy of the Bye Week is the Silence. Here is the template; craft it to your own allegiances. You are living in the New York area, and while you love the city, you hate its teams. You and a Philadelphia friend have tickets to see the Monday night Giants-Eagles game at Giants Stadium. The Eagles have just lost a heartbreaking game to the lowly Cardinals at the Vet. The Eagles are now 2–2, but they should be 3–1, leading the division. The Giants are 3–2, and the fans of both teams know perfectly well that whoever wins this game will win the division and have a shot at going to the Super Bowl. They also know that the losing team will quickly unravel and knavishly recede from the playoff picture. The Giants have beaten the Eagles nine games running, blitzing

Eagles quarterback Donovan McNabb into the earth's core. If you are an Eagles fan, the situation does not look good.

There are 78,000 drunken men at the game, and they are all wearing blue. You and perhaps 300 others are not. Worse, you are not drunk. As kickoff time approaches, the Yankees are polishing off the Seattle Mariners to win their thirty-eighth American League pennant. It is, on first glance, the complete New York Experience. On the overhead screen, the Giants management has seen fit to taunt the Eagles and their paltry faithful with images of Rocky Balboa being crushed by the home team's resident predator, Michael Strahan. The game begins, and for fifty-eight minutes and eight seconds, the Eagles stink out the joint. Their defense is porous. Their offense is pitiful. But the Giants cannot put them away. In the first half, they reach the Eagles' red zone five times but only come away with nine points.

The plot thickens.

Throughout the first half, the crowd is buoyant, optimistic, haughty. But as the game inches toward its conclusion, the faithful get nervous. God has given the Yankees what he always gives them, but he is never so generous with the Giants. God knows that if the Giants and the Knicks and the Rangers and the Jets and the Mets racked up as many championships as the Yankees, the Republic would totter and the wise man might very well purge himself with hysop. For starters. God, who graciously allowed the Giants to play in the Super Bowl the previous year, does not want this. Giants fans know this. With just under two minutes remaining, McNabb finds elusive wide receiver James Thrash in the corner of the end zone. Eagles 10; Giants 9.

The sound of 78,000 grown men not saying anything all at once is deafening. It's like the entire U.S. Marine Corps has come down with laryngitis. It is the Silence of the Spheres.

I am not the sort of person who goes to stadiums to root against the home team. In recent years, I have made innumerable trips to Philadelphia whenever I want to see the Eagles, Flyers, 76ers, or Phillies. I have no interest in pissing on somebody else's parade. When fans trek to other cities and get spat on and beat up by the locals, I shed no tears. You had no business being there. You got what you deserved.

But October 22, 2001, is special. The Giants' winning streak against the Eagles that began on August 31, 1997, is over. The Eagles have finally beaten Big Blue. To hear 78,000 screaming fans gagged by a spectacular game-winning play by a quarterback who is going to torment them for the next ten years is the very elixir of life. The Silence is the loudest sound in the entire universe.

Shortly after that memorable game, I was cleaning out my office when I came upon three totemistic objects that had managed to escape the Great Haberdashery Purge. One was a "Legion of Doom" T-shirt depicting the great John LeClair–Mikael Renberg–Eric Lindros line. I had bought it in 1994 and seemingly misplaced it. The second was a Phillies cap I purchased before my children were born. It was so old it had faded from red to maroon. The third item was a white, limited-edition *Philadelphia Daily News* T-shirt celebrating the 1993 Phillies' win over the Atlanta Braves. On the front was a full-color picture of Mitch "Wild Thing" Williams—scant days from forced retirement—leaping into the air after he recorded the last out in the game that brought the pennant to Philadelphia.

Discovering these precious talismans was more exhilarating to me than stumbling upon the Shroud of Turin in my mother's sewing basket. I have learned my lesson. The die is cast; the course is set. I am never, ever throwing away another piece of Philadelphia sports regalia. No matter how much disappointment lies ahead, I am never, ever throwing in the towel.

I am sure my teams will, however.

10

TRUE BELIEVERS

ON DECEMBER 2, 1997, I RECEIVED A DISTRESSING PHONE call from a doctor in a Philadelphia hospital informing me that my father was deathly ill. Seventy-two years of hard drinking, hard smoking, and generally hard living had taken their toll. The Grim Reaper was at the door, and he wasn't leaving unaccompanied.

In one of life's odd little coincidences, just as my father was heading into his grave, the Eagles were climbing out of theirs. The hometown favorites had started the season at 1–3 but had won two of their last three games after benching the undersized journeyman Ty Detmer and switching to the promising rookie Bobby Hoying. The plucky Buckeye immediately bested the Steelers, battled the Ravens to a fare-thee-well, and nipped the Bengals in an epic shootout with Cincy legend Boomer Esiason. These games seemed to usher in a new era, convincing the faithful that the Eagles would ride Hoying's mighty howitzer all the way to the Super Bowl. To this day, you can still see a few Eagles fans sporting teal-colored shirts with the name Hoying on the back. But I think they are being ironic.

As luck would have it, the Eagles were playing the dull, predictable Giants that weekend, and if they won the game they would be in first place and headed for the playoffs. As luck would have it, I happened to have a ticket to the game. As luck would have it, the game was to be played on December 7, the fifty-sixth anniversary of Pearl Harbor. As luck would have it, my dad, having served with honor in the South Pacific, had now come down with cancer of the spine, cancer of the lungs, cancer of the throat—the whole shooting match. Although the initial prognosis was that he had less than a year to live, this was the usual managed-care, cancer-ward hokum; it was extremely unlikely that my father would still be among the living come playoff time. Every time I showed up at the hospital in the last twelve days of his life, he had succumbed to yet another disease. At one point, when he asked, "How am I doing?" I told him, "You only need to get diptheria and pneumonia, and you win the Jeep Cherokee and the trip to Hawaii." The wisecrack elicited my father's last terrestrial chuckle.

Although I volunteered to skip Sunday's game, my father would not hear of it, insisting that he wanted to catch up on his beauty sleep. Like many people in his situation, he refused to believe that he was dying, and my going to the game or shooting back up to New York for a few days or buying him a dozen paperbacks was a way of reinforcing the illusion that his present indisposed state was but a passing phase. My father also wanted me to go to the game because he believed it would take my mind off his current misfortunes. This was the last in a lifelong series of defective theories. If you wanted to take your mind off impending tragedy, the Philadelphia Eagles were the last group of people to whom you would turn for solace. The Philadelphia Eagles *were* an impending tragedy.

Just because your father is dying doesn't mean that you stop watching football. And just because your father is dying doesn't mean your team will win. Working from the same script they had been using since 1960, the last time they won the NFL championship, the Eagles got creamed that Sunday. Of course, being the Eagles, they had to rub it in. Five days before my father died, the Eagles got knocked out of the playoffs by the traditionally meek Atlanta Falcons. Though they had lost the previous game to the Giants, there was still a chance they could make the playoffs if they won their last two games and a couple of other teams lost. I watched that game with my two oldest friends, Chris and Rob, and Rob's father, the gentlest, sweetest man I have ever known.

All through the game, as things looked tense, I told my friends to sit back and enjoy the game, assuring them that there was no way the Eagles could possibly lose. The Eagles would rise to the occasion; they owed me this one. Late in the game, an Eagles tight end dropped what would have been the game-winning touchdown, and the contest went into overtime. This was even better: drama. Then, without warning, disaster struck: An unheralded Atlanta receiver took the ball, broke about forty-five tackles, and rumbled forty-seven yards, setting up the winning field goal. We were all devastated. Of course, we had seen this kind of thing before, but Jesus, didn't the Eagles have any sense of occasion? After the game, when asked to explain their failure to come through for me at such a difficult moment, I had a simple answer: "Somebody down in Atlanta's got a father who's *really* sick."

I'm sure that my father wasn't all that thrilled about dying, but not having to hear about the Eagles anymore probably took some of the sting out of it. My father had always hated professional football; his pigskin passions—cheer, cheer for old Notre Dame—were actuated exclusively by ethnicity and religion. He liked pro basketball and professional ice hockey even less. Baseball was a different matter entirely; a peanut vendor at Connie Mack Stadium in 1950 when the Phillies won the pennant on Dick Sisler's three-run homer in the tenth inning, my father never stopped talking about the Whiz Kids, the single most beloved team in the city's history. Even though they got swept by the Yankees in the Fall Classic.

When he was very small, the Philadelphia A's fielded amazing teams that were every bit as good and perhaps better than the 1927 Yankees. But owner-manager Connie Mack broke up the team in 1932—as he had done in 1915, after a similar run—and the miserable franchise mostly finished in the second division from 1932 until 1954, when they finally left town for Kansas City. By the time my children were born, the Philadelphia A's, now having experienced an amazing rebirth in Oakland, had largely been written out of history. Every child knows about Ruth and Gehrig; no one under the age of forty has ever heard of Al Simmons and Jimmie Foxx. So it goes.

Anyway, my father, a Democrat, was a die-hard Phillies fan; the A's, like the Yankees, were the GOP squad. The A's had long since pulled up stakes, and so had the Republicans.

SINCE MY FATHER ONLY ROOTED FOR THE PHILLIES, NOTRE Dame, and Joe Louis, and only rooted for them when they were winning, we didn't engage in much sports bonding during my youth. When I was in my early teens, I would sometimes visit my uncle, Jim Burke, an insurance executive and Eagles season ticket holder who lived in a mildly prosperous suburb. Uncle Jim had a tape recording of the 1960 championship game against the Packers and would play it whenever I visited. He never tired of hearing the account of Ted Dean's go-ahead fourth-quarter touchdown but took the most pleasure from listening to Chuck Bednarik's game-saving, open-field tackle of Jim Taylor on the eight-yard line as time ran out. "You can get up now," said Bednarik, when the final gun sounded. "You just lost."

Years later, when I was finally browbeaten into reading Fredrick Exley's morbid, drastically overwritten novel *A Fan's Notes,* a book that has inspired more bad writing than *The Old Man and the Sea,* I struggled through the dense thicket of hyperbolic prose until page 347, when Bednarik put a murderous hit on the Giants' golden boy Frank Gifford. The hit was so hard it knocked Gifford out for the rest of the season and nearly ended his career. It was two in the morning, I was lying on my sofa as I was reading this, and I practically jumped out of my seat with joy. Bednarik's savage hit was the only part of the book I enjoyed. I wish he had hit Gifford even harder. In fact, I wish that he had hit Fredrick Exley before he had a chance to write his book.

When I was fifteen, Uncle Jim started taking me to an annual football game at Franklin Field. He usually invited me to games against the lackluster Cardinals or the dismal Saints. But I never forgot those outings, because something memorable always happened. In the Saints game, wide receiver Ben Hawkins, a stylish non-Philadelphia type who played with his chin strap dangling, caught touchdown passes all afternoon. And in the Cardinals games, free safety Larry Wilson repeatedly led the defensive unit on a series of outlandish blitzes. Other teams sent seven. Some teams sent eight. But the Cardinals seemed to be sending the whole team, half the bench, and most of the taxi squad. Every other down. It was like going to a circus where the elephants kept getting loose.

One afternoon I asked Uncle Jim if he had ever taken my father to a game. He laughed caustically and said that while he was still dating my mother, my father had gone out with him to the stadium and spent the entire afternoon ridiculing the Eagles. He said they were a bunch of lazy, no-good bums who couldn't hold the jocks of Glenn Davis, Doc Blanchard, Johnny Lujack, and all the other collegiate pigskin immortals. He said they were only playing for the money, that they didn't have the heart and passion of college players. My uncle told him that professional football players didn't need heart, because unlike college players, they had talent. But he assured him that the pros had heart, too. Heart in spades.

It was the only time Uncle Jim took my father to a game. It was also the year the Eagles won their first NFL championship. My uncle was so discouraged by my father's behavior that he considered telling my mother to call off the engagement, honestly believing that a man who didn't root for the Eagles would never make a good husband. Especially during a banner year like 1948. As things turned out, Uncle Jim was right. My father did not root for the Eagles. And he most assuredly did not make a good husband. To this day, I still believe that the two are connected.

My father had a streak of orneriness in him that makes a human barnacle like me look like St. Francis of Assisi. When Richie Ashburn, the Hall of Fame center fielder who saved the 1950 season by throwing Cal Abrams out at the plate in the ninth inning of the final game, died of a heart attack in 1997, I mentioned to my father that I had never met anyone who didn't like Whitey, far and away the most beloved Phillie of them all.

"I never cared for him," my father muttered bitterly.

"Why not?" I asked.

"I never liked his attitude."

For his career, Richie Ashburn hit .308, winning the batting title twice. Despite a weak arm, he led National League outfielders in put-outs, assists, and double-plays in the same season twice, leading the league in put-outs a record-tying nine times. His final season, when he was banished to the New York Mets, he batted .306. Even though he knew that he belonged in the Hall of Fame long before nonentities like Phil Rizzuto, he did not spend the rest of his life whining about it. In 1995, when the Special Veterans Committee finally voted him in, the entire Delaware Valley rejoiced.

My father never liked his attitude.

No wonder I turned out the way I did.

■ ● ■

AT A VERY EARLY JUNCTURE, IT BECAME APPARENT THAT my father was not going to make a very good role model for me, the budding fan. So I found others. At age nine I went to work for a former U.S. Marine drill instructor and Iwo Jima veteran who ran a bargain-basement, tumble-down clothing store in the starkly proletarian community of East Falls. Len Mohr was the most generous and most interesting man I have ever met. His father was the oldest living fireman in Philadelphia, a retired tillerman. Though a high school dropout, Len lived in a beautiful house in Bala Cynwyd, a twee suburb on the Main Line. There he would walk his Airedale every night, to this day my symbol of financial success. He had a picket fence, a pool table in the basement, a classy station wagon.

On the side, Len dabbled in the stock market, gobbling up high-flying but ultimately doomed "Nifty Fifty" stocks like National Video Corporation and Ling Electronics. He talked about the stock market all the time, insisting that you couldn't participate in the American dream without participating in the stock market, a view I share. He also was one of the original partners in Cloverlay, a group of well-heeled local businessmen that backed Joe Frazier on his way to the heavyweight championship of the world. And he refereed amateur fights at a North Philly gym called the Blood Pit.

As if all this was not enough, he also owned three parking lots right down the street from Connie Mack Stadium. On hot summer days when there wasn't much business at the clothing store, he would close up shop early and head over to North Philadelphia, where I would shoo cars onto the lot. Back in those days, there usually weren't many customers: Connie Mack Stadium was in the middle of the North Philadelphia ghetto, and the second year I worked for him the Phillies lost twenty-three straight games, a major-league record that will almost certainly never be broken. Round about the third inning we would wander up to the stadium to watch the rest of the game. It wasn't pretty.

A famous man once said that youth is wasted on the young. No longer young, I now understand that sentiment. When I was a little kid, I thought everyone owned three parking lots right down the street from Connie Mack Stadium. I thought everyone knew Joe Frazier. Because I was young and the world was new, I did not profit from my good fortune as much as I could have. I never attended any of his fights because by the time I was fourteen Muhammad Ali was the idol of every young American and Joe Frazier was the enemy, the white man's champion, the guy your dad rooted for. Thus, even though I worked for a man who had helped a slaughterhouse alumnus from South Carolina rise to the heavyweight championship of the world, I secretly rooted for Muhammad Ali.

My nonchalance about my good fortune did not stop with Smokin' Joe. Even though I got to meet all sorts of baseball players when they parked their cars for free on our lot, I didn't think all that much of that either. The Phillies were horrible, and baseball was not that big a deal back then. It was part of the fabric of life, sure, but in the same way that drinking milk or taking the trackless trolley was. I'd met Joe Frazier and parked cars at Connie Mack Stadium, and one of my classmates at Cardinal Dougherty High School was the Phillies' visiting team batboy. But it was no big deal. Not to me. Not back then. Back in those days, all I wanted to do was to get out of the housing project and become a famous writer and make a lot of money. Joe Frazier and the Phillies weren't going to help me do that.

My father didn't like Len. He didn't care for the gung-ho Marine Corps attitude. He insisted that the store was a "front," that the reason Len spent so much time on the phone was because he was a bookie. To me, that only made him seem even more exotic. But in truth what I liked most about Len was his passion. He never forgave Jack Nicklaus for blotting out Arnold Palmer's fleetingly radiant sun, and there were several members of the Phillies squad whom he despised with a venom that surpassed all human understanding. Len hated flashes-in-the-pan like Bo Belinsky, the sleek Angels lefty who pitched a no-hitter in his rookie year, dated Mamie Van Doren, and then, once it was apparent that he was a bum, was banished from glamorous Los Angeles to glamorless North Philadelphia. Len had no time for kooks (Bob Uecker), has-beens (Wes Covington), misfits (Dick Stuart), head cases (Dick Allen), or show-offs (Tony Gonzalez, Willie Montanez). But his greatest ire was reserved for guys who couldn't hit. And there was no one, anywhere, ever, who hit worse than Phils' shortstop Bobby Wine.

From 1960 until 1968, or so Len believed, Bobby Wine was always the man at the plate with the bases loaded, two down in the ninth, and the Phillies trailing by a run. A superb fielder with a cannon arm, Wine was one of the worst hitters of that or any other era. He played twelve years and batted .215, with 30 HRs and 268 RBIs. His best year was with the Montreal Expos, when he hit a poky .232 but drove in fifty-one runs. Len hated him. Hated him.

Frequently, he would tell a story illustrating the depths of his animosity. When baseball players turned up, we never charged them to park. One day, he recalled, a man with an instantly recognizable crew cut pulled into the lot, parked, and started to walk up the street toward the stadium.

"Hey, buddy, that'll be a buck and a half," Len called out.

The man turned around.

"I'm Bobby Wine."

Len didn't miss a beat.

"Hey, buddy, that'll be a buck and a half."

I, too, hated Bobby Wine. I hated his horrible stance. I hated his haircut. I hated his eternal linkage with the 1964 team that pulled the biggest choke job in the history of American sports. Everything I loved about baseball I learned from Len, and everything I hated I learned from him too. Boy, did we hate Bobby Wine.

Ah, but baseball is a game of redemption. When I was a little boy, I once stood outside the locker room at Connie Mack Stadium and tried to get Robin Roberts's autograph. Roberts was not available. Neither were any of the other stars. So I got an autograph signed by a dud pitcher who won only three games that year, and won only twenty games in his entire career. He was a loser. He was a bum. Twenty years later, he would lead the Phillies to their one and only championship. His name was Dallas Green.

God knows where the autograph is now.

The summer of 1987, I was given four tickets to see the Astros and Mets play a doubleheader at Shea. The teams had battled each other tooth and nail the previous season in one of the greatest series in the history of the game, but this season was different. The Mets, the defending National League champs, weren't going anywhere fast, and the Astros weren't going anywhere faster. The seats were directly behind home plate, allowing me to chat with the guy who operates the JUGS Gun. One of my guests was a friend from England, who didn't know anything about the sport. I spent much of the first game regaling him with stories about the good old days at Connie Mack Stadium. I tossed in the Bobby Wine story for good effect. The punch line got a nice laugh.

In the second inning of the second game, I looked across the railing separating me from the next box and saw a middle-aged man with an instantly recognizable crew cut. It was Bobby Wine. We got talking. He said he was now a scout for the Atlanta Braves and was here on business. I asked him why he had never been given a shot at the Phillies managing position after spending so many years in the organization. He was philosophical about it; he wrote it off to politics. The Phillies, predictably, had treated one of their own shabbily. It was widely known that when Dallas Green led the Phillies to the championship in 1980, Bobby Wine was a sort of surrogate manager, an *éminence grise.* He was also adjutant to Paul Owens when the Phillies won the pennant in 1983. He had started his major league career as a shortstop who simply could not hit, and had ended it by helping the Phils win two pennants in the space of four years.

I asked him for his autograph. He signed the back of a business card. I sure hope he wasn't sitting there when I told that story about Len Mohr and the parking lot.

I have a few autographs in my office collection. Red

Auerbach. Bobby Hull. Billie Jean King. Bobby Nystrom. Jim Palmer. Once, after I rescued Julius Erving from a bunch of gawking rubes ("So, Irving, how tall *are* you?") at a March of Dimes event in Manhattan, he signed a copy of the *New York Daily News* ("Doc Gets His Ring" was the headline) and handed me a Cabbage Patch Kid Doll for my daughter. But of all the autographs I have collected, the one I value the most is Bobby Wine's. Wine's injury-plagued career illustrates what is best about sports, that there is always tomorrow, that hope springs eternal, that if a determined man can't get in through the door, he'll come in through the window. You just have to keep that window open for about twenty years or so.

WHEN I WAS YOUNG, I PROMISED MYSELF THAT I WOULD never write about sports because then something that I loved would become work and gradually morph into something I hated. But this was stupid. At some level, I already do hate sports. It has ruined the better part of my life, consuming vast amounts of time and money, promising glittering rewards that inevitably turn out to be fool's gold. What I have learned in the end is what I suspected in the beginning, that being a fan is a lot like smoking: a bad habit you pick up in your early teens and can never quite break. To me, the Phillies and the Eagles are exactly like nicotine: a preposterously noxious semihallucinogenic substance capable of giving great pleasure for brief periods of time, but that will ultimately destroy your health.

Richard Ford once wrote, "If sportswriting teaches you anything . . . it is that for your life to be worth anything you must sooner or later face the possibility of terrible, searing regret." Sports fans love to spend time that should be used raising their families or advancing their careers lamenting what might have been. Red Sox fans will never let go of Bill Buckner's muffed grounder in 1986. Mets fans will forever wonder what would have happened had Mike Piazza gone after Roger Clemens when he threw the bat at him in the 2000 World Series. Tennis fans bemoan the derailing of Monica Seles's career by a deranged fan in 1993. I personally have spent between three and five years of my life wondering why Wilt Chamberlain, the greatest player of all time, took only two shots in the second half of the last game of the 1968 Eastern Conference finals, his final appearance in a Sixers uniform.

Just what have I gotten out of sports in the past twenty years? Not a whole lot. Waxing poetic about the good old days with Smokin' Joe once kept me from getting my head demolished in a seedy South London pub, but other than that the larder is pretty bare. Like a cabal of wily Ottoman eunuchs, my teams have schemed, conspired, and colluded to make my adult life an uninterrupted string of heart-wrenching disappointments. The Mitch Williams home run. Lindros's six concussions. Assorted Eagles tank jobs. Assorted Sixers tank jobs. Twenty years without a championship in any sport. Whatever happened to the law of averages?

In the end, I have been left with nothing but some colorful team photos and a handful of unequivocally fine memories. Yet, oddly enough, my happiest, most priceless experiences do not involve championships. In 1978 I attended the game where Pete Rose broke the National League record for consecutive games with a first-inning single. But until I unearthed a giveaway poster from the game squirreled away in my no-hope chest, I had completely forgotten I was there. Pete Rose was a Red when he got the hit; no accomplishment by any player from another team would loom as large as an event involving my own teams.

Not that said event has to involve a championship-level contest. In 1999 I realized that I had never been to an Eagles game with my friend Rob. We had seen countless Phillies games, numerous Flyers games, and had once gone to a 76ers game specifically to see Kareem Abdul-Jabbar, who got thrown out of the contest when it was only a couple of minutes old for throwing the ball at the referee. It was the only basketball game we ever attended together, and the only time either of us ever saw Kareem Abdul-Jabbar in person. We got to see him take one shot. Thanks a lot, Big Fella.

The 1999 game pitted the Eagles against the Redskins. The Eagles were suffering through a typically disastrous 5–11 season with a new coach, and were massive underdogs. The Eagles were so pitiful that they benched their starting quarterback, Doug Pedersen, on this, the tenth game of the season and went with an untested rookie. His name was Donovan McNabb.

The Redskins, loaded with nimble running backs and fleet receivers, and guided by the crafty Brad Johnson, scored in three plays on their first drive. Then they scored in four plays on their next drive. By the end of the game, the Redskins had amassed 424 yards in total offense. But the Eagles fought back. Buoyed by six takeaways, they went ahead in the fourth quarter and were leading 35–28 with time running out. On the last play from scrimmage, fourth and something, everyone in the stands knew that the Eagles were going to blitz. Everyone on the field knew that the Eagles were going to blitz. For all I know, Brad Johnson may have known the Eagles were going to blitz. But he never saw the blind-side blitz coming. He heard it, though. Sixty-five thousand screaming people were on their feet as a black-and-teal projectile came tearing through the backfield. Johnson hit the ground with a thud, the clock ran out, and the Eagles had won. Massive underdogs to our second most hated rivals, we had come from behind with out kiddy-car offense and baby-faced quarterback who, we were now all sure, would lead us to the Promised Land. I had witnessed the most memorable game in my life—the dawn of the Donovan McNabb era—with my two closest friends and the durable, incomparable, vastly underrated Joe Weiss. It was exquisite. It was heavenly. It was beyond belief.

But maybe you had to be there.

Mr. Weiss is still coming to the games with us. But only after a close call. In game 4 of the 2001 season, the Eagles were leading the entirely unnecessary Arizona Cardinals by 20–14. The home team had played atrociously, quickly falling behind by fourteen points, but had rallied to go ahead in the fourth quarter. Now the Cardinals had the ball with a little more than a minute to play, no time-outs, and eighty yards to go. A hopeless predicament, one might say. But spurred by Jake "the Snake" Plummer, who, like most football players with colorful nicknames, is a complete bust except when he is playing the Eagles, the Redbirds covered fifty yards in four plays, then scored the winning touchdown when All-Pro Troy Vincent fell down on the five-yard line while trying to make a game-saving tackle. All this happened in the right-hand corner of the end zone, directly below our seats.

We took this hard. But nobody took it harder than Mr. Weiss. A season-ticket holder in the 1960s and 1970s, he had stopped going to the games when the Eagles started charging fans for meaningless preseason games, games so bad that the drunks who painted their faces got the colors wrong. Now, at the age of eighty, he made the pilgrimage only once or twice a year. It was unfortunate that this outing had to be one of them. As we emerged from the subway in Center City, Joe's face went completely white and he collapsed outside an Italian restaurant. We all thought he was a goner. Think of it: the Eagles were now not only breaking our hearts; in Mr. Weiss's case, they were literally causing cardiac arrest.

The EMS people whisked Joe off in an ambulance. Rob and I followed on foot. We stayed at Thomas Jefferson Hospital until four in the morning, eating very bad food from the local Wawa's. There was the usual cock-up about tests, EKGs, medicine. No one could say exactly what had happened. On the overhead TV, the local stations were replaying the highlights of the game. Things were looking grim. But they didn't stay that way. By the next morning, Mr. Weiss was fine. The doctor put it all in perspective: Mr. Weiss was no spring chicken, it was boiling hot, he hadn't eaten all day, and the Eagles had just blown a game they absolutely had to win. He had simply fainted.

Needless to say, the Bye Week was coming up.

Announcers and pundits always like to say that near tragedies help to put sports into perspective, reminding us that they are merely a diversion. They've got it backward. Sports put tragedy in perspective; life is the diversion. Being a real fan is the stuff of life itself. It is the ongoing quest for the municipal Holy Grail. It is the implacable fight for justice. It is the honest belief that today will be better than yesterday and tomorrow even better than that. So if you were entering your ninth decade, and a passionate fan, and your number was up, what better way to go than at a football game?

Obviously, you would have preferred that the home team won.

ONE OF THE GREAT THINGS ABOUT SPORTS, AS ANY CHILD will tell you, is that there is no script. If there were, North Carolina State would never have beaten Phi Slamma Jamma, and there would have been no Miracle on Ice. If there were an underlying symbolic logic in the sports cosmos, the Yankees and Mets would have met in the 2001 World Series, after bin Laden did his number on the World Trade Center, and not in the Fall Classic of the previous year. Instead, the Mets missed the playoffs, and the indomitable Yankees were beaten on a fluke hit, a broken-bat flare to shallow left dinked by a player who had done nothing for most of the Series, an underachiever playing for a team that lost $30 million that year. It's worth remembering that Rudy Giuliani was at that final game in Arizona, just as he was at the season-ending game when the Giants lost to the Eagles. The closest he got to a victory was at the 2002 All-Star Game, which finished in a tie. This would seem to demonstrate that baseball is a great sport but a terrible metaphor. It also shows that God stubbornly refuses to stick to the script. As do the New York Mets.

During the Eagles' lugubrious 3–13 season in 1998, I asked

my friend Rob if there were any circumstances under which he would stop being an Eagles fan.

"No," he replied, not even considering the question.

"Why not?" I asked.

"I like pro football," he said.

I like pro football, too. I like pro football more than I like porterhouse steaks, Ludwig van Beethoven, gay Paree, and huge paychecks. I like pro football more than my career, more than my pension fund, more than the Microsoft stock I bought at twelve bucks, more than life itself. I like pro football more than life itself because in my experience pro football provides more thrills than life itself. And I feel the same way about pro basketball, professional ice hockey, and major league baseball. I love these things because they provide an exhilaration that cannot be found anywhere else, and because they moor me to my youth, my family, my friends, and the city of my birth.

At the ripe old age of eighty-two, my mother has unexpectedly developed a crush on Donovan McNabb and insists that my sister tape the games every Sunday so she can watch them when she gets back from winning 2,400 nickels at the Taj Mahal. Then, on Monday morning, she calls me to discuss the games. Mind you, she doesn't know much about safety blitzes or double reverses and couldn't tell a full-house backfield from a power sweep. But she's learning.

In 1972, when I was twenty-one years old, I went to Paris for a year. It was, without question, the happiest year in my life, the touchstone experience I return to again and again. Museums. Alcohol. Cathedrals. Alcohol. Beautiful French, Finnish, Dutch, and Japanese women. But mostly alcohol. Well, alcohol and all those Canadian nurses living in my *pension*.

Residing in that Parisian boardinghouse were a Canadian couple named Skip and Judy Angel. Skip liked ice hockey more than he liked breathing. The boardinghouse was also home to a Yugoslav army officer who adored the Soviet hockey team, the gang of professionals who masqueraded as amateurs until the International Olympic Committee finally put an end to the charade. That winter, the Russians were playing the Canadians in a historic eight-game series. It was the first time anything like this had happened. The Soviets, ridiculed by the Canadian media, stormed in and thumped the locals in their heretofore inviolate shrines and went back to Russia with a 2–1–1 lead. Soon, it was 3–1–1.

One night, before the tournament had resumed in Moscow, Skip came down to the kitchen where the Yugoslav and his wife were eating.

"Best hockey teams in the world," snorted the objectionable spawn of Tito, counting on his fingers. "Number one, Russia. Number two, Finland, Number three, Sweden."

Then he went back to eating his gruel.

Skip didn't say anything. There wasn't much to say; the Canadians were on the ropes. But over the next few days, the series tightened up. The Canadian goal-tending clicked into gear. Flyers center Bobby Clarke hobbled the Commies' best player with a typically vicious stick across the ankle. Maple Leafs winger Paul Henderson went on a scoring tear. The following Sunday, the Canadians won 6–5, taking the series 4–3–1.

That night, I was sitting in the basement having dinner. The Spanish tenants were there. Ditto the Venezuelans. The Yugoslav army officer was over in the corner, reading *Le Figaro.*

Skip came down the stairs, grabbed a drink, stood directly over the soldier.

"You want to run those hockey rankings past me again?" he said, with a smile as wide as the Canadian Great Plains.

Before I die I want to wear a smile like that.

Recently, I began a rigorous self-improvement exercise program. I cut out the ice cream, stopped driving to work, started running again. I could have a good, long wait until the Phillies, 76ers, Flyers, or Eagles reward my efforts. I want to give them lots of room to work with. If I can just live another thirty years, it is almost beyond the realm of mathematical probability for my teams not to win anything. I have run the numbers.

ALL GOOD SPORTS STORIES END UP IN CHICAGO. NEW York may be the sports capital of America, and Philadelphia is my beloved hometown, but if you really want to understand the psyche of the sports fan, you have to go to Chicago. And much as I commiserate with the long-suffering fans of the Chicago White Sox, all good sports stories lead to Wrigley. It is the temple. It is the basilica. And even though I hate to use the word, it is the *cathedral.* It was in the cathedral in the summer of 2001 that a complete stranger made the most acute observation about sports that I have ever heard. I had come to the stadium because I wanted my son to see Wrigley for the first time. The Cubs immediately jumped all over the Buckos: 5–0 after one; 10–2 final. With Sammy slugging a line-drive homer over the left-field wall not thirty yards from where we were sitting.

Late in the game I wandered out for some bratwurst. Spotting a very old man nibbling on what seemed to be a very old hot dog, I politely asked how long he had been a Cubs fan. His entire life, he replied; he was from the North Side. The Cubs were four games in front that late July evening, but they would collapse, as they always collapsed, come August. The man was at least seventy-five; he hadn't seen the Cubs in the World Series since Harry Truman was president; they hadn't actually won the Fall Classic since Tinker was tossing the old horsehide to Evers and Chance, two decades before he was born. He definitely had that Vladimir and Estragon look about him. The guy had been through the meat grinder.

I fired off my next question. "Forgive me for asking, but what's it like to spend your whole life rooting for a team that hasn't won a World Series since you were born?"

He could have taken it as a taunt. He could have dismissed me as a typical, wise-ass New Yorker. Or a thoughtless, tactless tourist. Or just another front-runner. Or even a first-class jerk. Backed into a corner, he could have trotted out the usual Chi-town spiel about the mythical allure of Wrigley, about how every game was a movable feast, a celebration of our beloved national pastime. You know, the Ken Burns routine. But he didn't. He scooped up his hot dog and beer and started to vamoose. Then he looked back, smiled, and spoke with the peerless eloquence of the common man.

"Well, they've been playing pretty well lately," he said. "I think the inning's starting."

ACKNOWLEDGMENTS

The author wishes to thank Jennifer Barth, Martin Beiser, Joe Vallely, Ruth Kaplan, Hella Winston, Eliot Kaplan, Chris Taylor, Jennifer Pradas, Gino Salomone, and Gordon Queenan.

ABOUT THE AUTHOR

The author of seven previous books, including the bestselling *Balsamic Dreams* and *Red Lobster, White Trash, and the Blue Lagoon,* Joe Queenan is a contributing editor at *GQ* and writes regularly for *The New York Times, Forbes,* and *The Wall Street Journal.* He lives in Tarrytown, New York.